THE FALKLANDS:
South Atlantic Islands

THE FALKLANDS:
South Atlantic Islands

IAN J. STRANGE

Photographs and map by the author

DODD, MEAD & COMPANY
New York

PHOTOGRAPH CREDITS

Miss Madge Biggs, page 129, 133 (top); F.E. Cobb, 19, 20, 22-23, 25, 99, 104, 106, 126; Mrs. Crist, 123; Unknown photographer, 21. All other photographs are by the author.

Distributed in Canada by
McClelland and Stewart Limited, Toronto
Manufactured in the United States of America
1 2 3 4 5 6 7 8 9 10

Library of Congress Cataloging in Publication Data

Strange, Ian J.
    The Falklands: South Atlantic islands.

    Includes index.
    Summary: Looks at the history and present state of the
Falkland Islands through the eyes of a naturalist who
went there to live.
    1. Falkland Islands—History—Juvenile literature.
2. Falkland Islands—Description and travel—Juvenile
literature. 3. Natural history—Falkland Islands—
Juvenile literature. 4. Strange, Ian J.—Juvenile
literature. [1. Falkland Islands] I. Title.
F3031.S875 1985   997'.11   85-1458
ISBN 0-396-08616-0

To my many American friends who have an affection for the Islands. Especially Jeannie, Duffy, Anne and Michael, Diane, Cliffy, Andrea and Winty, and Helen. May you all return.

ACKNOWLEDGMENTS

My special thanks go out to the late Mr. F. E. Cobb who gave permission for the publication of many of his early photographs and also to Miss Madge Biggs for the use of some of her collection and for information about other early photographs which appear in this book. Grateful acknowledgment is also made to the Falkland Islands government for allowing me to extract details from the archives, to the original publishers of *Snow's Voyage to the South Seas and Tierra del Fuego, 1857,* and to Mrs. Bertha Dodge for an extract from *Marooned.* My thanks also go out to the many Islanders who over the years have added so much to my love and knowledge of these Islands. Last but not least to my wife, Maria, for typing a number of drafts and to Rosanne Lauer for her help and patience.

CONTENTS

1. INTRODUCTION

Wild and unspoiled areas of the world had always fascinated me, and probably this image of the Falkland Islands was what drew me to them in the first place. What little I could find written about the area presented me with a picture of a somewhat bleak, treeless expanse of tundra-covered islands. The Falklands consist of two main islands and some 340 islands and islets, set deep in the South Atlantic some 340 miles northeast of the notorious Cape Horn. Except for large numbers of penguins, a sheep-farming industry run by a small population of some two thousand inhabitants, largely of British descent, and connections with a long-past shipping route around the Horn, it seemed, according to my information, that there was little to look forward to.

The rugged, natural beauty of a Falkland coast. Much of the Islands' coastline remains unspoiled and a haven for wildlife.

As an agriculturalist in England, I had been asked whether I would like to go to the Falkland Islands to set up an experimental farm. With the image already in my mind of these Islands, the decision had soon been made and I was on my way. The project was for some five years, but what I was to find in these wild and primitive islands exceeded all expectations and my work was to change. That was twenty-three years ago and I am still looking for and finding new attractions in this small group of fascinating islands.

For three days the ship on which I was traveling had followed a course parallel to the South American mainland. Out of a blue, cloudless sky, the sun penetrated the sea breezes and kept temperatures around the lower seventies. On our last day at sea, however, there was a noticeable cooling of the wind. Although we still had a clear sky, the sea about us, at one time blue, had a much deeper, blue-green coloration. Bird life, earlier on the trip sparse, was now prolific. Albatrosses wheeled and dipped in the wake of the vessel, along with numerous other forms of seabirds with which I was still unfamiliar. My first feel of the Islands came when we were still some hours away. Quite dramatically, there was a new smell to the wind. Apart from the rich sea smell coming from some forms of seaweed, there was a distinct sweet scent to the air. This pleasant fragrance, I was to learn later, came from the dwarf shrubs and grasses that cover the Islands, a scent unique to the Falklands. Soon after, the horizon was marked by silhouettes of low-lying hills which designated the northern limits of the main island of East Falkland. At first the coastline was only a ribbon of gray which slowly developed into a formidable array of cliff faces intersected with beaches of the most dazzling white

The north coast of East Falkland, an array of cliff faces intersected with beaches of fine white sand. A group of elephant seals lie among piles of rotting seaweed.

Jason Islands

Carcass Is

Keppel Is

Saunders

West
Point Is

Hill Cove

WEST FALKLAND

Roy Cove

Port H

Chartres

New Island

Beaver Is

Weddell Island

Fox Bay East

Port Stephens

Speedwell Is

SOUTH ATLANTIC OCEAN

FALKLAND ISLANDS

SOUTH ATLANTIC OCEAN

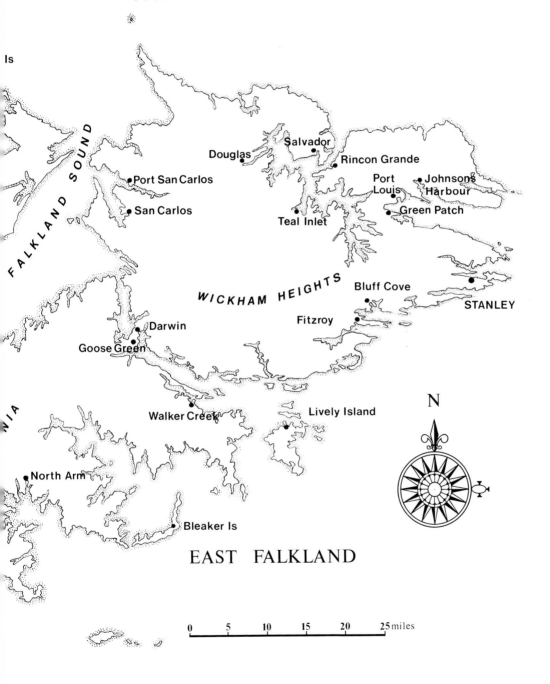

Is

FALKLAND SOUND

Salvador

Douglas

Rincon Grande

Port San Carlos

Port Louis

Johnsons Harbour

San Carlos

Green Patch

Teal Inlet

WICKHAM HEIGHTS

Bluff Cove

STANLEY

Fitzroy

Darwin

Goose Green

Walker Creek

Lively Island

N

NIA

North Arm

Bleaker Is

EAST FALKLAND

0   5   10   15   20   25 miles

sand. As a backdrop to these beaches, rich green expanses of fine grasses contrasted with the white sand. Further inland still, the greens gave way to a rich patchwork of rust reds, buffs, dark greens, and grays.

In some parts the coast was deeply indented, appearing to take the sea inland and giving one an urge to follow its course and discover what lay at the head. The navigational chart showed names such as Rincon de los Indios, Cape Bougainville, Black Point, Wineglass Hill, Macbride Head, Eagle Hill: an interesting mixture of French, Spanish, and English names which to me made the scenery even more interesting. I wondered what the history was behind these names. Traveling along the coast of East Falkland, our destination was Port Stanley, the capital of the Falklands. Entering Port William, the outer harbor to Stanley, the only sign of human habitation was a lone lighthouse standing at the point of a sand dune-covered cape. In style, the lighthouse had the appearance of those which guard the entrance to Scottish sea lochs. This became understandable when I learned that it had been manufactured in Britain at the turn of the century. The light itself was still operated with paraffin lamps and a revolving clockwork system.

With only fifteen minutes to go before docking, there was still no sign of a town. Ahead lay a narrow waterway which opened up into another harbor. After passing through these "Narrows," the town of Stanley was suddenly unfolded before us. On the shoreline of this almost landlocked harbor, the town was built across a gently sloping hillside, going down to the water's edge. Brightly painted, corrugated-iron roofs on the houses added a bright splash of color to the gray rock ridges that formed the tops of the slopes behind the town.

Stanley, capital of the Falklands. The red brick and stone structure of the Anglican Christ Church Cathedral lying close to the harbor is almost at the center of the town.

In its own informal way, Stanley was strangely geometrically placed. Lying parallel to the harbor, and across the slope of the hill, were a number of streets with neat rows of houses. Intersecting and running from the top of the town to the harbor front was another series of roads, thus dividing the town into small blocks. Almost at the center of the town, a large red brick and stone structure, the Anglican Christ Church Cathedral, dominated the scene. No matter which angle the town was viewed from, the focal point remained

A group of islanders awaits the docking of the RMS Darwin in Port Stanley.

the church and its clock tower. Even the tower and roof of the cathedral were clad in corrugated iron, but these blended in well with the design of the building and the surrounding town dwellings. I later learned that originally the design of the church had been that of a typical English church, complete with a spire, but in the final stages the Austrian stonemasons had declined to build the spire and the church tower thus acquired a roof.

Although our voyage had brought us eight thousand miles from England to a completely different hemisphere, I was wondering if the whole journey had not been a dream and we were instead only a relatively few miles out to a Scottish isle. The scenery was certainly reminiscent of such an area, and now that we were docking, many other familiar sights were before me. A crowd of people on the jetty was shouting greetings to fellow passengers, in a manner no different to what I would have expected had I been arriving back in England. The two police officers and the customs official wore the familiar blue uniforms of England. Land Rovers and other recognizable forms of transportation lined the road to the jetty.

As I scanned the array of buildings before me, a description written over one hundred years earlier by Captain Parker Snow took me back in time. Snow, then commander of the mission schooner *Allen Gardiner*, had made the same journey and entered Stanley Harbor as I had, to a place that had changed only superficially.

Stanley had a very pretty appearance from the harbour, with its double row of pensioners' white cottages, and the other light-coloured houses contrasting with the dark background. Seated on the slopes of the hill with one or two buildings of stone and brick conspicuous, and running along the side of the harbour for about three-quarters of a mile, it is, in itself, a rather attractive little place, considering the part of the world it is in. In front of the town are a few piers and jetties— the latter private, the former, one belonging to the town, and called the stone pier, the other a government pier, and fixed at the dockyard, which is at the western extremity of the town and known by the flag hoisted on

The pensioners white cottages described by Captain Parker Snow with the barracks, the larger building, at the end of the row.

arrival of a vessel, as also by the guard house, block-house, stores, workshops, etc. erected there, the whole railed in. Behind the dockyard is a reservoir of water to supply shipping; and far away, towards the head of the harbour are the government offices, gardens, stables, servants' houses, and the residence of His Excellency. This latter building is utterly unworthy of the name Government House and though looking pretty enough when viewed from the water, with its long unique cottage-like appearance, it is so low in dimensions and so undignified that it would seem to be more suitable for offices than for a residence.

Captain Parker Snow went on to describe Stanley further:

The Falkland Islands Company stores and buildings are at the extreme east of the town; and opposite to them, at anchor in the harbour, is their little fleet, consisting of one barque, three schooners, and several boats, cutters, etc. besides a large receiving hulk. The colonial manager's house, a verandah-cottage, is in the middle of the town, facing a private jetty; and I should observe that most of the principal houses face the harbour, from which they are separated by the best and almost the only road fit to walk upon in the colony. From the town pier, a street, so-called, leads up to the top of the hill. On the right and left of this street and running along the side of the harbour in front of all the houses, is Ross

The Falkland Islands Company stores and offices at the east end of the town about 1880.

Government House about 1887.

Road . . . .This road is nearly two miles long, its limits being a little beyond Government House at the one end, and in 1856 at the Cemetery Chapel at the other end.

Parallel with Ross Road, at the back of the first line of houses, is another very narrow street which runs through the town only as far as it was originally laid out. The houses facing this street are of inferior description. Some of them are occupied by men and their families engaged in the seal fishery; others belong to the Spaniards and those foreigners that are employed principally by the Falkland Islands Co.; but the best of them higher up the hill are owned by the handicraftsmen of the town, some of whom are not only solid men, but no doubt could, if they chose, come home with tolerable means of comfort. Most of these houses are built of stone and timber, brick being so excessively dear that it cannot be thought of. A few of the older tenements are made of wood, one or two being regular shanties, that is, patched up, cabin-like boxes. Walking along Ross Road we observe a public house on the left, kept by a Mr. Murray; and next to that, one of the most compact and pretty houses in the town, belonging to Mr. Bowden, who had newly built it just before I left. The Church, on a raised space by itself, comes next. Beyond the church are a few wooden houses, then comes the private house of Mr. Dean, the storekeeper, banker, agent, etc., then his store; next another wooden house, occupied by the family of one of the company's employees; then the cottage of Mr. Havers; next the surveyor-general's and then the colonial surgeon's, which is here at the corner of another small street, binding the principal part of the town. This last house, and several of those I have named, are very comfortably built and well furnished. Dr. Hamblin's garden is conspicuous for its flowers.

After a slight break we come to the Eagle Hotel kept

The Ship Hotel about 1880, formerly the Eagle Hotel described by Parker Snow. The colonial surgeon's house lies to the left of the hotel.

by Mr. Goss. Then another break and we come to the clergyman's residence, which is a very poor place by itself. Beyond this, upon the road, there are no more private houses; the dockyard etc., being now on the right, the police court and magistrate's abode, a little further on to the left up the hill. About here Ross Road descends a little, takes a turn over a small bridge trav-

The west end of Stanley in 1887 and the house of Captain Packe, one of the first sheep farmers in the Islands. Note the hulk of the East Indiaman *at the end of the jetty.*

22

ersing a diminutive stream and then proceeds straight on
to Government House. Turning back however we now
walk up by the police court, a couple or so of wooden
buildings, the prison being on the dockyard, and by a
pathway ascend to the rows of pensioners' cottages. As
we pass them, kindly greetings show that there are
warm and friendly hearts within; nor are those greetings

from many a rough hand and many a woman's tongue on an occasion just before I left Stanley forgotten by myself or my wife.

In the middle of the foremost row stands a large barrack-like building, with the central part a storey higher than the rest of it. I believe that formerly it was used as a barracks for the pensioners till they got their cottages. It stands in a conspicuous situation and has a very pretty view over the whole harbour and entrances. The pensioners' cottages look neat and one or two I was shown into were really patterns of household management. The total number of buildings in Stanley I should consider to be about a hundred, taking round numbers. Of these, many are really very comfortable, well furnished residences. Only a few are two-storeyed, and these mostly newly-built ones.

Even after a period of one hundred years, many places and individual buildings described by Parker Snow were there and very much in use. The modern-day successors of the "little fleet" were at anchor offshore, while some of those described by Snow, their working lives at an end, lay as hulks along the foreshore. Few tracks or pathways remained. The streets and roads were now paved with concrete or tarmac but still restricted to only a few miles. Outside Stanley, routes to the outlying settlements were no more than tracks across the "Camp," accessible only to vehicles such as the Land Rovers. All the countryside outside Stanley township is known as the Camp, from the Spanish *campo*, meaning countryside.

As I walked around Stanley, following in the footsteps of

Parker Snow, it became even more difficult to believe that I was so far away from England with its villages. Road signs bore the same symbols. Red pillar postboxes with Royal Cipher, the same emblem used by the British postal system, were placed in different parts of the town. Neat gardens displayed lupins, roses, fuschia, and many other familiar flowers, while vegetable plots grew cabbages, carrots, onions, potatoes, lettuces and, in more sheltered spots, peas. Much to my surprise, vegetables such as French and runner beans were absent. I soon realized that due to the predominant winds and the narrow temperature range, such plants were not able to grow. This also meant that pollinating insects, such as bees, were unable to survive.

To understand something of the weather in the Falklands

Typical style Falkland house in the late 1800s. This form of construction and style has changed little.

one must learn a little about their position in relation to the large landmass of South America. Lying to the east and in the lee of the southern part of the South American mainland, the Falklands experience some of the warming and drying influences of the Andes, the backbone of that continent. However, these effects are modified by the separation of the archipelago from the mainland by three hundred miles of relatively cold water. Westerly winds, which sweep across these waters from the Andes, give the Islands a cool, oceanic climate. The temperature range is narrow. Summer temperatures average 50° F, although in a sheltered spot out of the predominant winds—which average twenty miles per hour—temperatures can rise into the lower 80s. Contrary to the general belief that winters in the Falkland Islands are gripped by Antarctic conditions of snow and ice, the average winter temperature is 36° F, with temperatures rarely falling below 18° F. However, snowfalls have been recorded in every month of the year, but even in winter these are generally light, rarely putting a thin cover over the ground for more than a few days at a time. In Stanley the average rainfall is about twenty-five inches, similar to many areas of England. Although weather statistics gathered in Stanley do give a general picture of the Islands' climate, conditions do vary quite a bit from area to area. Generally speaking, the farther west one travels, particularly to the western edge of the archipelago on the outer islands, there is less cloud and therefore a tendency for more sun and a lower rainfall.

2. A WEALTH OF WILDLIFE

When the Islands were first sighted by early voyagers, reference was made to the thickly wooded nature of many of the smaller offshore islands. Almost certainly what these early navigators saw were the tussock-covered islands. Forming a dense cover over the ground, this grass, *Poa flabellata*, commonly attains a height of some six feet (two meters). Individual plants form stools, or bogs, as they are locally known, from the top of which grows a mass of green leaf. The bog forms from a mass of dead leaf litter and roots, as the growing point slowly increases in height. Seen from a distance, these bogs, topped with a mass of green leaf, would no doubt have given the impression of thickly wooded lands.

Tussock grass presents a strange contrast to the predominantly tundralike vegetation which covers a very large part of the Islands' landmass. It is also unique in that it usually

grows only in areas where it is subjected to sea spray and where it may benefit from the nutrient-rich droppings of seabirds and seals.

Before man settled the Islands and introduced stock to the two main islands of East and West Falkland, tussock grew on coastal points and some coastlines of these islands. But cattle, horses, and subsequently sheep, attracted to this very nutritious and palatable grass, quickly destroyed it and today very little tussock remains on the main islands. The smaller islands and islets, largely inaccessible or just too small to make them worth stocking, were left untouched, except for occasional ravages by early sealers. Today many of these islands are still covered with a dense growth of tussock grass and probably remain in much the same state as when man first saw them.

Visiting a tussock island is an experience few people forget. Once in a thick stand of tussock one enters a different world. Even with a strong breeze blowing and a chill in the wind, there is calm and warmth amidst the stools or bogs. Although not always evident as one first approaches one of these

Left: Stands of tussock grass growing on the edge of the shoreline where it benefits from sea spray and the rich nutrients from seabirds and seals.

Right: The dense and deep growth of tussock grass.

islands, they are rich in bird life. Not only do the bogs and leafy growth afford shelter for nesting, but there is also an abundance of food for insect-eating species.

Of the sixty-three breeding species of birds found in the Falklands, a very large number are either seabirds or species which rely directly on the sea for their survival. The variety of species is not great, but numbers of individual forms are very large. Penguin species, of which there are five found in the Islands, run into several million birds. The small rockhopper penguin—probably the most common species— has an estimated population of some 5 million. The alba- trosses, shearwaters, and petrels, a group collectively known as tube-nosed birds (Procellariiforms), also nest and live about the Islands in very large numbers, the offshore islands holding vast colonies.

During the spring and summer months some of these is- lands become alive with the swift-flying forms of petrels. However, only a night's vigil on a breeding colony can give an idea of the extent of the populations. During the daylight hours these birds spend their time at sea feeding but, as the last light disappears over the horizon, they close in on their breeding grounds. Sitting on a darkening island waiting for these birds to return to their nest burrows is an experience which never fails to impress me. There is always that feeling, as darkness descends, that the birds will not appear. Then suddenly, one is aware of a few light forms swiftly darting to and fro—these will be prions, a form of petrel, their delicate blue-and-white coloration showing against the dark- est of skies. Within minutes the numbers grow, with the sound of fluttering wings adding to the scene. Finally, when all the returning birds are circling over their breeding ground,

Large colony of black-browed albatrosses and rockhopper penguins on an outlying offshore island reserve.

the impression is that of being in a snowstorm. Gradually the petrels drop to their individual underground burrows located, it is believed, by scent. A very characteristic musty odor can be detected on every petrel colony. It is then that one becomes aware of the extent of some of these colonies. A sound not unlike the noise of a great waterfall, as birds greet their mates, rises up from hundreds of square yards of land. This sound continues until dawn when the birds, as quickly as they appeared, leave their burrows and return to the sea.

To breed and reproduce, birds need suitable breeding grounds. The Falklands, and in particular the smaller, tussock-covered offshore islands, present these grounds. The birds are able to dig burrows in the bases of tussock bogs or plants. But of greater importance is a readily available supply of food within a reasonable distance of these breeding areas. As an offshoot of the great Southern Ocean Current, which flows east with the West Wind drift past Cape Horn, the Falkland Current bears a cold stream northward to the Islands. On reaching the archipelago, the current's flow is split, one stream going east, the other to the west, these dividing again into many small tidal streams as they pass among the islands. In these areas the otherwise great depths of this current are sharply reduced by underwater ridges, which cause great tidal action and an upwelling. The effect is a natural funneling of marine life to the surface, where it becomes more readily available as food to these vast colonies of seabirds and seals.

One of the most important forms of food is *krill*, a collective name given to the shrimplike Euphausians and a form called *Munida*, lobster krill. Krill forms vast food fields which build up in the region of the tidal streams and upwelling, so dense

In some parts, stacks and bluffs form some of the Islands' most impressive scenery.

Above: Teal Inlet on East Falkland is a typical medium-sized farming community, with sheep raising for wool the prime occupation.

Below: Stanley, the capital, is characterized by wooden houses, clad with brightly painted corrugated tin roofs.

Typical islanders, descendents of British stock who came out to settle the Falkland Islands in the mid-1800s.

Above: Present Governor or Civil Commissioner of the Falkland Islands, Sir Rex Hunt CMG, in the typical ceremonial uniform for a governor of a British colony.

Left above: A short-eared owl in a typical habitat of tussock grass.

Left: Black-browed albatross with its newly hatched youngster.

Above: A small breeding colony of king penguins.

Below: Rockhopper penguins drying themselves after coming ashore.

Typical scene on the southwest corner of the Falkland archipelago: Sea cliffs on the west side of New Island, which in some areas drop five hundred feet into the sea.

Although modern forms of transportation are taking over, the horse is still very popular with many islanders.

that the water appears pink from the creatures' coloration. Traveling in these areas of the sea, one is made aware of the great importance of this readily available food. Groups of penguins porpoise in the turbulent waters alongside fur seals feeding on shoals of krill, while terns, gulls, albatrosses, and petrels take food from the surface. Often in these areas, rafts of albatrosses numbering tens of thousands of birds can be seen for periods of several days taking food from one such food field until winds, tides, and currents finally disperse it. At the height of breeding, these birds and larger species of penguin may take over two pounds of food per day to their young.

Just how important these food fields are to the Islands' wildlife, and the vast quantity of food required daily to sustain these populations, became apparent to me when I made my first visit to a large breeding ground. Landing on the lee of the island, the air was still and yet there was the unmistakable stench of a seabird colony. Making my way through the thick tussock grass which covered a large area of the island, I approached the opposite coast guided by a roaring sound which I took to be the sea. Breaking through the outer tussock fringe, I stood hardly believing the sight which lay before me. Amassed along this coast was a colony of black-browed albatrosses and rockhopper penguins so densely packed that it would have been impossible to walk through without stepping on either birds or their nests. What I had taken to be the roaring of surf was in fact the discord from this enormous rookery. Later, with the aid of aerial photography and ground surveys, it was calculated that this vast colony held a population of albatrosses numbering 2 million birds; the number of penguins exceeded this figure.

It was such sights that convinced me to remain in the Falklands at the close of my agricultural project and to make the study of the wildlife and its conservation my primary objective. Besides a lifelong interest in such things, I felt that there was a great need for someone to study the Falklands' wildlife and record their findings for, although naturalists had worked in the Falklands before, there was still a great deal to be learned. It amazed me that the sort of sights I was to see about the Islands were unknown to the world outside and sometimes unknown to people living in the Islands themselves. Some species of birds were only to be found in the Falklands; some, like the striated caracara, were rare and in need of conservation. This raptor or bird of prey is both scavenger and predator of penguin and other seabird colonies, feeding on eggs, young, and dead or diseased birds. Locally it has the curious name of "Johnny Rook." My first experience with these raptors was on a large gentoo penguin colony. Standing about the rookery, waiting for a chance to take the eggs or young from an unwary penguin, these birds reminded me at first of rooks standing about a field in England. The name "rook" was commonly used by early sealers when describing this hawk, while the name "Johnny" was given to the gentoo penguin.

Other scavenging and predatory species living off the huge rookeries of penguins and albatrosses are sheathbills, dolphin gulls, skuas—which, although capable of taking food directly from the sea, are commonly seen about the colonies picking up waste food which penguins and albatrosses bring ashore for their young.

Approaching the Falklands by sea, often long before the Islands themselves are sighted, one will note a scent of sea-

The striated caracara or "Johnny Rook," one of the Southern Hemisphere's rarest birds of prey in a habitat of tussock grass.

Rockhopper penguins coming ashore through thick beds of kelp seaweed.

weed and large rafts of kelp will be seen floating on the sea's surface. These rafts come from the vast beds of kelp which grow in the offshore waters of practically every coastline in the archipelago. So common are these beds that the islanders have acquired the nickname of *kelpers.*

The term "kelp" can refer to several species of seaweed found growing in different areas closer inshore. In the deeper waters a true kelp, brown seaweed, known by the name of

Macrocystis pyrifera (which, strangely, also grows off the coast of California), is perhaps the most impressive. Its long growing strands reach thirty yards in length. Beds of this kelp cover many square miles of inshore sea areas. Closer inshore, and often exposed at low tide, are beds of tree kelp, a form known as *Lessonia* and also one known as *Durvillea*. All these kelps, with their thick stems and leaves and the ability to move and stretch with the action of the sea, not only act as a physical buffer against pounding waves preventing many shorelines and smaller islands from being eroded away, but they also play an important part in the ecological chain. The

Adult pair of flightless steamer ducks.

beds shelter many forms of marine life, which in turn become important feeding habitats. The Islands' flightless steamer duck, the crested duck, and the chiloe widgeon are all marine-feeding ducks. When beds of tree kelp become exposed at low tide, night herons probe the shallow pools beneath the thick cover of the kelp for food.

Behind the buffer of this kelp lies yet another area closer inshore where the more delicate and softer forms of seaweed grow, such as sea lettuce and another, brown-leaved kelp known as *Iridea.* Kelp geese graze these forms, and at certain times of the year the upland geese will come off their usual grass "greens" to feed on the kelps.

Two species of geese are common to most regions of the Falklands, the upland goose and the ruddy-headed goose, the former being more abundant. For most of the year these two species of geese feed on greens, rich areas of grassland which predominate the coastal edges where freshwater ponds and streams abound. In the Southern Hemisphere seasons are reversed and therefore the Falklands' autumn is during March and April. During these fall months, when the berries of dwarf shrubs such as diddle-dee and teaberry ripen, the geese may leave their usual feeding grounds to feed and build up a reserve of fat for the winter by eating the berries.

In contrast to the richly populated coastal regions, the interior of the main islands supports little bird or animal life. Among the hilly, rugged areas of No Mans Land of East Falkland, such as Wickham Heights, only the occasional scream of a red-backed buzzard, chatter of a carancho (or crested caracara), and the song of a few passerine or perching bird species indicate that any bird life exists in these areas.

When man first arrived on the Falklands' shores he dis-

Kelp geese, the all-white male and intricately patterned female.

covered, besides the large numbers of seals, only one true land mammal. This was the Falkland wolf or a *warrah*, a large wolflike fox which closely resembled the South American jackal (*culpeo*). Soon extinct at the hand of man, many questions remain unanswered about this curious creature and the fact that no other land mammals were discovered. I believe that the Falkland wolf was never a native or indigenous creature but a late introduction to the Islands—perhaps by some mistaken voyage of Fuegian Indians, or on one of their canoes. It is well known that these people used tamed culpeos as hunting dogs and carried them in their boats.

Adult pair of upland geese, a common grazing species.

3. THE ISLANDS ARE DISCOVERED

A certain amount of controversy will probably always reign over the question of the discovery of the Falklands. Some historians consider that the first sighting of these remote islands was made by the Florentine navigator Amerigo Vespucci about 1502. There is also the possibility that one of Magellan's ships could have sighted the group. Camargo's expedition, which reached the Straits of Magellan in 1540, also reported the finding of several islands, the description of conditions, land, birds, and seals being similar to the Falklands. However, it is generally accepted that the first unquestioned discovery was made by the Elizabethan navigator John Davis, whose vessel, the *Desire*, was driven among the Islands on August 14, 1592. Two years later Sir Richard Hawkins in the *Dainty* also reported finding the Islands, which he named Hawkins Maiden Land. In 1600

One of the Jason Islands, originally named the Sebald de Weert after the Dutch navigator who recorded them in 1600.

three of the outer islands, in the northwest corner of the archipelago, were sighted by the Dutch navigator Sebald de Weert. He gave his name—the Sebalds—to those three particular islands which are today known as the Jason Islands.

The first undisputed landing which is well recorded was made by John Strong, commander of the British vessel *Welfare*. Strong sighted the archipelago on January 27, 1690, and made a landing. The *Welfare* spent six days sailing around, with Strong naming the stretch of water between the two main islands (now East and West Falkland) Falkland Sound. Viscount Falkland was the First Lord of the Admiralty at that time and eventually his name was given to the whole group.

In 1701 the French navigator Gouin de Beauchene made a landing and also discovered the most remote island in the group, which today still bears his name. The French called the archipelago Isles Malouines, after St. Malo, from where many of their expeditions to the South Seas set forth. The French were to remain at the forefront of Falkland exploration. Finally the young French nobleman Antoine Louis de Bougainville, viewing the prospect of a new colony in the Malouines, decided to establish a settlement there and thus lay claim to the Islands for France.

De Bougainville had two ships, *Eagle* and *Sphinx,* especially prepared and in September, 1763, loaded with a large variety of supplies, seeds, and plants, he set sail from St. Malo with a crew and settlers numbering about 140 persons. Supplementing their cargo with cattle, pigs, goats, and poultry at Montevideo, Uruguay, the little expedition finally sighted the Islands on January 31, 1764. On February 2, the two ships anchored in what is today known as Berkeley Sound.

Beauchene Island discovered by the French navigator Gouin de Beauchene in 1701.

Some weeks later the site for their new settlement was chosen at the head of the Sound. A fort of clay and stone, an apartment house, and some turf huts were erected and on

The Carenage at Port Louis and site of the first settlement established

April 5, 1764, a ceremony of possession took place. The fort was to be called Fort Saint Louis and the settlement eventually was named Port Louis.

Today the original foundations of the little fort and its surrounding buildings are still visible, overlooking the wide

by Louis de Bougainville in 1764.

open waters of Berkeley Sound but snug alongside a small, almost landlocked harbor, with a backing of rolling hills. Even today, standing among the old foundations, one can visualize the amount of activity which must have beset the scene—men busy constructing the fort, while women and

47

children were no less active tending their newly acquired stock, preparing gardens, and turning sods of peat. The records of the expedition's botanist, Pernetty, tell us they discovered peat as a fuel shortly after their arrival. On reflection, this was a discovery of immense importance to the future settlement, for no other fuels were to be found. Although the expedition must have been anxious about settling this new and unknown land, one can conclude from Pernetty's writings that hopes were high for the success of their venture. But changes were to follow.

When Spain heard of the new settlement, she protested the French occupation and in 1766 de Bougainville agreed to transfer the little colony to the Spanish government on payment of "618,108 livres 13 sols 11 deniers," a sum of £25,000. On April 1, 1767, the possession was formally handed over to Spain.

While de Bougainville was establishing Port Louis, preparations were being made in England for a voyage of exploration to the same islands, under the command of Captain John Byron. His instructions were to survey the Falkland Islands. On January 15, 1765, Byron entered the harbor which de Bougainville had named Port de la Croixade almost a year before. This was at Saunders Island—an island lying to the north of West Falkland—which Byron named Port Egmont in honor of the First Lord of the Admiralty.

Byron claimed Port Egmont and adjacent islands for George III in complete ignorance of de Bougainville's claim on behalf of France. A few days later Byron set sail and continued his survey along the northern limits of the Islands, eventually coming to the entrance of the wide sound on East Falkland which he named Berkeley Sound. Had he entered, the now

A scene on West Falkland a few miles from Port Egmont, the first British settlement established by Captain McBride in 1766.

established French settlement would have been discovered. However, due perhaps to an unfavorable wind or tide, Byron elected not to enter and thus remained ignorant of the French occupation. After Byron's departure from England, rumor was to circulate that the French had already occupied the Falklands and in September 1765, an expeditionary force composed of three ships—the *Jason, Carcass,* and *Experiment*—sailed from England for the Falklands under Captain John McBride.

McBride arrived at Port Egmont on January 8, 1766. Almost a year later, on December 3, 1766, while exploring the east coast, McBride sighted the French settlement. The following day he visited the commander, de Nerville, now in charge of the settlement, and informed him of Britain's claim to the Islands. At this time, however, both parties were unaware that de Bougainville, having returned to France, had agreed to hand over France's rights to Spain.

Early in 1767 McBride returned to England, leaving Port Egmont under the command of Captain Hunt of the *Tamar.* On the opposite side of the archipelago, Port Louis, now renamed Port Soledad, was under the command of the Spaniard Don Felipe Ruiz Puente.

In September, 1769, Hunt, cruising in *Tamar,* came across a Spanish schooner from Port Soledad. Hunt presented the master with a formal warning to leave the Islands, but a few days later the matter was reversed, when on a second meeting Hunt was presented with letters from Puente ordering the British to leave the Falklands or, as the Spanish called them, Islas Malvinas. More letters were to pass between the two commanders, each issuing notice to the other to leave.

The situation was not to improve. Finally a confrontation

of the small British force against overwhelming forces of Spanish at Port Egmont resulted in the British raising a flag of truce. Under articles of capitulation the British surrendered the settlement on Saunders Island to the Spanish, and on July 14, 1770, the small force left to return to England, having been purposely delayed so that the news might first reach Buenos Aires and Spain.

The two countries almost went to war but finally negotiations resulted in an order for restitution being signed on February 7, 1771. A few months later the small fort and establishment at Port Egmont were again taken over by a British commander. Three years later, however, the British abandoned the settlement—an action which is still raised in dispute over the ownership of the Falklands.

Until 1806, the Spanish maintained the settlement at Port Soledad, but it was never to be a great success. In 1806 turmoil came to Buenos Aires and on hearing that the British had occupied that city, the Spanish governor of the Malvinas quickly abandoned Port Soledad and fled to Montevideo. Four years later revolution was to result in the separation of Spain from her South American colonies, but the Spanish governor of Soledad was never to return to his post and thus Spain's jurisdiction over the Falklands lapsed.

From 1806 to 1820 the Islands were completely abandoned by all forms of authority. Whalers, sealers, and privateers used the archipelago to their liking. Several of the well-sheltered island harbors, at New Island, West Point Island, and others, became self-styled homes of these men. Even the former seats of authority at Port Egmont and Port Louis were taken over by these exploiters. Besides the seals and whales which were being taken, the crews of passing vessels found the Islands a useful place for replenishment of supplies. Wild geese and the eggs of penguins were a valuable addition to their stocks, but probably of greater interest were the increasing numbers of wild cattle and pigs which now roamed the East Falkland mainland from the original animals introduced by de Bougainville.

On November 1, 1820, formal rights of possession were declared in the name of the newly created United Provinces of the River Plate, and three years later the first Argentine governor to the Islas Malvinas was appointed. In that same year of 1823, the United Provinces made a grant of thirty leagues of land, with cattle and fishing rights, to Louis Vernet. Vernet, a Frenchman by birth, previous merchant of Hamburg, and South American by naturalization, had great plans for creating a colony in the Islands. By 1831 Vernet had established some ninety settlers at Port Louis engaged in fishing and dry salting beef which he marketed in South America. In 1828 Vernet was granted rights to the entire East Falkland and on June 10, 1828, was appointed governor of the Islas Malvinas and Tierra del Fuego.

In protection of his fishing rights, Vernet attempted to prevent foreign vessels from continuing with their previously uninterrupted sealing about the archipelago. On July 20, 1831, he seized the North American sealing vessel *Harriet*, along with two other vessels. His actions were eventually to bring reprisals and in December of that year the United States corvette *Lexington*, commanded by Sylas Duncan, took revenge by sacking the settlement at Port Louis. To Vernet, absent from the Islands at the time, it was a great blow to his work and aim to establish a "great national fishery." He was never to return to the Falklands.

In September, 1832, a temporary governor took over—Juan Esteban Mestivier. His office came to an abrupt end when he was seized and killed by a number of mutineers. Confusion again reigned over the possession, when suddenly there arrived at Port Louis the British ship HMS *Clio* under the command of Captain John James Onslow. Onslow had arrived, according to the letter issued to Don Jose Maria Pinedo, then in command of Soledad, "to exercise the right of sovereignty over these islands." To Pinedo it was an insult and, although he agreed to leave, he refused to strike his flag. On January 5, 1833, he sailed for Buenos Aires aboard his vessel *Sarandi*.

A few days later Onslow left, leaving the British flag flying over the settlement. Now in charge was William Dickson, an Englishman who had previously been employed by Louis Vernet as a storekeeper. A few weeks later the *Beagle*, commanded by Captain FitzRoy, called at Port Louis. The then young naturalist Charles Darwin was on board and both he and FitzRoy were dismayed at the state of the settlement, in which whalers, sealers, and gauchos took full advantage of the absence of authority. During the visit of the *Beagle*, Captain Matthew Brisbane, being the senior British resident, took charge of the settlement.

Brisbane made an effort to bring law and order to the community and salvage Vernet's business. However, many of Vernet's labor force, which composed part of the remaining community, were Indian convicts. Having had a taste of freedom, they were unwilling to return to law and order under Brisbane and on August 26, 1833, eight of them attacked and murdered Brisbane, Dickson, and three others. The remaining settlers—thirteen men, three women, and

53

two children—escaped to Turf Island in Berkeley Sound.

Yet again the little settlement at Port Louis was to add to its history another taste of violence and disorder, but it was to be the final chapter. On hearing of the murders, HMS *Challenger*, which had previously been given orders to call at the Falkland Islands, set off from Rio de Janeiro and on January 9, 1834, arrived at Port Louis. On the following day, Lieutenant Henry Smith was installed as governor, and a long period of uninterrupted British administration had finally arrived on the Islands.

4. A NEW COLONY

About 1828, British Lieutenant William Langdon, who commanded the vessels *Hugh Crawford* and *Thomas Laurie*, had visited the Falklands. Sailor and sheepfarmer, Langdon probably saw prospects for the Islands and with an associate, G.T. Whitington, obtained from Vernet grants of land on East Falkland. When Britain took possession of the Islands, Whitington hoped that with the grants obtained from the Spanish governor he might continue a similar business. Reports of the lush grasslands and the speed with which cattle reproduced and fattened on the Islands probably gave Whitington great hopes for the development of agriculture. In 1834, he formed the Falkland Islands Commercial Fishery and Agricultural Association and forwarded a prospectus to the British government. He was, however, sadly disappointed by the reaction, as approval for his scheme was not granted. To have done so would have meant recognition of

Vernet's claim on the Islands and, indirectly, that of the Buenos Aires government. Whitington then applied for new rights to land on the Islands, offering to colonize and pay for an expedition and for the salary of a governor who might be named by the Crown. The British government continued to disregard his proposals until finally Whitington's brother, J.B. Whitington, set sail for the Islands with eighteen other people who were prepared to settle. That same year the Colonial Land and Emigration commissioners in England proposed that the Islands be colonized, and on August 2, 1841, Richard C. Moody, aged twenty-eight years, was appointed in London as lieutenant governor of the Falkland Islands.

Moody was left to plan his operations and by October of that year he had gathered together a small party and supplies. A brig, the *Hebe*, under the command of Captain Anderson, which was at the time being prepared to go to the Falklands, was able to accommodate Moody's little expedition. On January 15, 1842, the 190-ton *Hebe* anchored at Port Louis. Before Moody departed from England he had been informed that the Lords Commissioners of the Admiralty believed that Port William, fifteen miles south of Port Louis, would be safer and more convenient as the port for use by Her Majesty's ships. Moody's thoughts as he sailed up the wide entrance of Berkeley Sound toward the small entrance into Port Louis must have been dominated by His Lordships' words. He would have noted that the prevailing westerly winds, which swept down the Sound, did make entrance for their sailing ship, if not difficult, certainly a long task. At the head of the Sound there were islands which had to be negotiated before a vessel could anchor safely. Even then, it is most probable that before landing in the inner harbor, the right wind and tide had to be chosen. The inner harbor, or Carenage as it is still called, is approached through a narrow seaway opening up into a small, snug, almost circular area of water. The land around the Carenage hardly reaches an elevation of more than fifty feet but, with the harbor being so small, it affords good shelter. Even today, one can visualize the scene before Moody as he entered there. Standing on the highest point overlooking the Carenage was the low stone building built by Vernet which was now to be Government House. Alongside was another stone structure known as the Barracks. Some distance over the meadows, on another prominent position, were the ruins of the turf and stone French fort, and nestling for shelter along the lower-lying foreshore, an assorted array of stone, turf, and timber buildings—eight in number—belonging to the few settlers of that time. Cows, pigs, horses, and recently introduced sheep brought in by Whitington roamed around the area of the little settlement, the whole, as Moody was to describe it, looking like some Cumbrian seacoast village.

Between the years 1834 and 1842, the Islands had been supervised by a British naval superintendent and a small naval party. Their tasks had been to keep law and order and to see to some of the administrative duties. Reading through the log books that were kept at the settlement, the impression is that rather than a civil administration, the few settlers were embraced very much in naval traditions. Musters were held every Sunday, the articles of war read, and wrongdoers apparently subjected to naval discipline.

On January 22, 1842, under a salute from HMS *Sparrow*, at that time stationed in the Islands, Moody officially landed

Teal Inlet settlement north of East Falkland.

at Port Louis and took over from the naval superintendent, Lieutenant John Tyssen.

Had Moody continued his voyage down the east coast of East Falkland, past the entrance to Berkeley Sound and Port William, he would have come to the entrance of an even larger sound. Known as Choiseul Sound, it sweeps to the northwest and almost dissects the East Falkland mainland into two sections, only a narrow isthmus at Darwin joining the two. To the south side of the Sound is a great plain known as Lafonia, which only in a few areas rises more than one hundred feet above sea level. To the north he would have noted that the coastal areas were not unlike those that he would have seen on his voyage down the east coast of East Falkland, still relatively low lying. But a few miles inland the landscape changes, sweeping up to form a long range of hills which curve across this northern section of the mainland from west to east. Known as the Wickham Heights, they form a formidable barrier of broken-topped hills with a maximum elevation of just over two thousand feet. At the western end of this range is the Falkland Sound and the almost landlocked harbor of Port San Carlos; at the eastern extremity of the Heights lies Port William.

Before Moody had made his official landing at Port Louis, he had already visited Port William and, with the assistance of Lieutenant John Tyssen, examined the area and the harbors with a view to establishing a site for the chief town. In a report back to Lord Stanley, Moody expressed the opinion that Port William was much better adapted as a site for the proposed chief town, but felt that due to the lateness of the season it was advisable for him and his party to remain at Port Louis temporarily. Following instructions from Lord

Stanley, Moody made further investigations at Port William. By then, however, it was the onset of winter and he reported his concern at the very wet state of the area and that he considered Port Louis a more favorable site. At this time the Ross Antarctic Expedition was anchored at Port Louis, and Moody asked Captain Ross for his advice on the selection of Port William as the new town site. Again sites were selected at Port William and on the inner harbor of "Jacksons Harbor"—now Stanley Harbor. Moody was still doubtful and reported to London that he had laid out positions for a new town at Port Louis which he proposed to call Anson. The idea was to make Anson a "temporary principal town" awaiting the growth of the colony before building another. Moody was clearly enthusiastic about the future of the Islands and their capacity to survive on their own natural resources. He made many sound, practical suggestions which were probably based on his own and the settlers' experiences at Port Louis. However, his plans for Anson were not favorably received by the Colonial Land and Emigration Commission and, probably backed by naval authority, the commissioners wrote to Lord Stanley: "We have expressed our conviction that the site of the capital should be fixed at whichever port should be decided by competent authority to afford the greatest advantage to shipping. The report from Captain Ross will we should apprehend to be considered as conclusive upon this point." In March, 1843, Lord Stanley wrote to Moody saying that he objected to any arrangement of a temporary nature and that he was to move and establish a new seat at Port William.

In the midwinter month of July, 1843, work began on the new town site, Moody having selected the north-facing slope of the present-day harbor and the position of the present-day town. For Moody and his small detachment it must have been a most daunting task, surrounded by some of the wettest and roughest land in the Islands. On the credit side, as Moody reported, the area offered vast deposits of peat which was required as fuel. In August, 1843, Moody commenced to move the seat of government to the proposed new town site, where he had constructed a turf hut and a small wooden cottage. But progress was slow and it was not until August 16, 1844, that the first official letter bore the name Stanley. This was written by Lord Stanley suggesting the name for the new capital. Officially the town came into being on July 18, 1845.

The construction of the new town started with two wooden cottages, a smithy of sod, brick, and clay, a storehouse and carpenter's shop, some of which still remain almost in their original form today.

Soon after Moody had commenced his move from Port

Stanley Harbor about 1890.

Louis to the new town site, he received from London the Charter under the Great Seal for the Constitution of the Government of the Falkland Islands. At the same time, he received the commission and instructions for his appointment as governor and commander in chief. Both documents were dated June 23, 1843. It was not until April 2, 1845, however, that Moody was able to form an executive council, with the colonial surgeon and colonial magistrate and Moody himself as members, and a legislative council later in the year, with the magistrate and Moody's brother—who had arrived as chaplain—as the unofficial member. Moody's task of establishing a basis for the future colonization of the Islands was not easy. Administrative support was lacking, and this had made it difficult for him to form his legislature. Whitehall's view was that he should lead the settlers by example, yet he was hampered by insufficient financial support from the British government to implement many of his plans. (Whitehall is the term for the British government, its offices, or policy. It is on a London street named Whitehall where many government offices are located.) Moody was also hampered in his task of founding a new colony by the generally unruly seafaring community around him. The period from 1806 until the 1830s had been one when there was little authority in the Islands and during which whalers, sealers, and privateers used the archipelago as they liked. The influence set up by such men no doubt continued and it was some years before authority was able to control the situation. Governor Rennie followed Moody and, in an attempt to bring some order to the colony, he formed a magistrate's court. Many offenses became punishable by law. He also attempted to apply the law to the coasts of the Falklands, an action that very nearly brought Britain and America to war.

By 1850 the new colony had become well established under British sovereignty but its status was often unknown or casually ignored by foreign whaling and sealing crews who continued to go about their exploitations. In 1853, concerned about continuing plunder, in particular by American vessels, the British government notified the United States that it intended to post a naval force in the Islands to prevent this. The United States accepted this and in turn issued a notice to the masters of their vessels bound for the Falklands which warned them of the penalties. Depredations continued, however, and in March, 1854, Governor Rennie reported to London on the circumstances which had led to the arrest of one Captain Hiram Clift, master of the American whaling vessel *Hudson,* and of a Captain Eldridge of the tender vessel *Washington,* both of whom had been heavily fined earlier for killing cattle on East Falkland. In his report, Rennie wrote:

> In the beginning of January last, six deserters belonging to the above vessels arrived in this port in a boat which they had stolen from the *Washington.* They deposed before Mr. Montagu, the Magistrate, that they left the *Hudson* moored in Ship Harbour, New Island, serving as a depot for the *Washington* which was employed to capture whales within the headlands of these Islands, this being the season when whales come near the shore to produce their young. That while so employed Captains Clift and Eldridge had killed a large number of hogs belonging to the Falkland Islands Company on Saunders Is. and likewise destroyed a great many seals

on the Government rookeries. They also stated that for about 8 months the crew, amounting to thirty-six men, had lived entirely on pork and geese killed on the Islands.

At the time this information came to Governor Rennie, he had no vessel in which to proceed to New Island to arrest Clift and Eldridge. He immediately wrote asking for naval assistance but, before his request could have been delivered, there arrived in Stanley the HMS *Express* under the command of Captain Henry Boys, who had been dispatched by the British government to assist Rennie in the matter of the plunderings.

Living in Stanley at this time was William Smyley, the American sealing captain who had the self-declared position of United States commercial agent. At about the same time that Rennie wrote asking for naval assistance, Smyley sent a letter to the American consul in Montevideo informing him of the measures to be taken against his countrymen. Shortly after the arrival in Stanley of the HMS *Express*, the manager of the Falkland Islands Company took out a warrant for the arrest of the American masters on a charge of pig killing, and the *Express*, with the chief constable aboard, was dispatched to New Island to apprehend the two culprits. Smyley's information to the American consul in Montevideo brought an immediate reaction with the dispatch to Stanley of the American corvette *Germantown*, a vessel of 1,000 tons with an armament of 16 long, 32-pound and 6 long, 64-pound cannons. The *Express* was only 360 tons and armed with six 32-pound guns.

The *Germantown* arrived in Stanley Harbor on March 2.

On the next morning the schooner *Washington* arrived, followed a few hours later by the *Hudson*, accompanied by HMS *Express*. The commander of the *Germantown*, Captain Lynch, seeing that his countrymen's vessels were under arrest, "beat to quarters and shotted his guns," which, according to Rennie "in sight and hearing of a small settlement totally defenceless naturally created alarm to the inhabitants." Shortly after this action by the *Germantown*, Rennie was visited by Smyley and Lynch who wished to know for what cause and by what authority the two whaling captains had been arrested. Rennie informed Lynch of the nature of the charges and produced a copy of the notice which had been issued by the United States secretary of state to masters of vessels bound for the Falklands. Lynch denied that the notice applied to this particular case and disputed Britain's rights over the cattle or pigs on the Islands. The warrant was illegal, he protested, and he, Lynch, could not permit his countrymen to be tried. To this Rennie replied that in view of the amicable relations existing between their two countries the decision of the Court of Justice should be awaited. Rennie wrote:

> Captain Lynch refused to adopt this course, still asserting the illegality of the arrest and that he would not have his countrymen brought to trial. My reply was in words to this effect: that whilst I lived, notwithstanding the overwhelming force at his immediate disposal, I would never permit him or anyone to dispute the authority with which I was legally invested by Her Majesty to administer the Government of this Colony and to uphold the law.

66

Captain Clift appeared in court a few days later and on his own confession was convicted of unlawfully killing twenty-two pigs for which he was fined. The day before the trial, the *Germantown* moved her anchorage, mooring immediately in front of the court house and, as Rennie reported, during the whole day of the trial, "The tompions were out of eight of his guns, generally indicating that the piece was loaded, and from the situation of his vessel they pointed direct at the Court House"—an act which Rennie considered could only be an attempt to intimidate the course of justice.

The matter was not closed for some years, and on the return of Clift and Eldridge to the United States a document was drawn up claiming damages for the two owners of the vessels *Hudson* and *Washington,* amounting to $39,000. The bill eventually was presented to the British government twelve years later, in 1866. In 1854, the United States secretary of state wrote to the British minister at Washington complaining of Rennie's action and asking for compensation. However, when the documents relating to the case were eventually printed in 1871, the whole matter appears to have been forgotten in the large amount of material concerning the Alabama Claims which arose during the American Civil War.

The move from Port Louis to the new town of Stanley had not met with total approval from the settlers. Whitington wrote: "Of all the miserable bogholes in the Falkland Islands I believe Mr. Moody has selected one of the worst for the site of the town." However, by the end of 1844, most of the settlers had moved to the new site. Early in 1846 it was reported that work had begun on the construction of roads and drains, three jetties built, and a seawall constructed along the front of the town site. That same year 164 persons resided in the town, which was then composed of fifteen cottages, twelve houses, and three huts.

At Port Louis, development of the agricultural pursuits was slowly forming through the work of settlers like Whitington. Besides these, Stanley required the development of the other interests needed in a growing capital. One of the government's hopes had been for colonization by private enterprise, but this had been disappointing. In October, 1849, there did arrive at Stanley a detachment of marines together with thirty army pensioners, their wives and families, who had been offered the opportunity to make a new life in the Islands.

The youngest pensioner was twenty-six years, the average age forty-two. Life as a pioneer settler after a barrack life such as they had been used to was a lot more than some could endure. Many had been pensioned off from the army life due to injuries, which must have added to what many found a difficult life. Prefabricated cottages had been brought out for the pensioners and still remain today as two neat rows of dwellings flanking a central building known as the Barracks, as described by Parker Snow. The attempt at settling the pensioners was not a complete success; many were to return to England. Five families stayed and became established as excellent gardeners or tradesmen, with many of the descendants of these families remaining in the Falklands today.

With the increasing population, many of them children, education was a matter of increasing importance. However, it was not until 1860, when there were 117 children of school age in Stanley, that the first qualified teacher was appointed.

In comparison with the number of inhabitants at that time, the number of children receiving education in Stanley today is not much higher, just over two hundred in 1980. How many children were in the Camp in the year 1860 is not recorded, but today there are some 135 children receiving education in Camp schools or houses. For those children in the more remote settlements, and particularly those living in what were termed "outside houses" or shepherds' establishments, often many miles from any other habitation, education has from the beginning had problems. Such children relied solely on traveling teachers, often the clergy. Traveling by horse, and covering many settlements, meant that children often saw their teacher only a few days in many weeks.

When the little colony was first being established, the church and school were closely connected in more than one sense. In October, 1847, Moody reported that a wooden building had been erected in Stanley to serve as a church and school building. A shortage of buildings and higher priorities in the early days resulted in both church and school being moved from pillar to post. Shortly after Moody's report, it was recorded that the same building was now hospital and dispensary. In 1852, at the request of Governor Rennie, a large stone building was started with a central tower and two wings. Originally built as a public marketplace and referred to as the Exchange Building, it was completed in 1854. Soon after it became the temporary residence of the governor. By 1856 this was changed again, one wing becoming the church, the other a school. Eventually in 1862, the building took on the name of Holy Trinity Church. In 1872 when Bishop Stirling, first Bishop of the Falkland Islands, visited the Islands, he refused to consecrate the building while one half was being used as a school. So proposals were again made to move the school and thought was given to the building of a proper church. Services were, however, to continue in the Exchange Building for some years with no move being made to build a new church. One night the situation was to change quite dramatically.

The difficulty of carting peat prompted the early settlers to cut their peat as close to the town as possible. The system was haphazard and little attention was given to draining off the old workings. Being situated on the brow of the hill immediately at the top of the town, accumulated water gradually increased the pressure on that area of uncut peat that divided the town from the peat workings. On the night of Friday, November 29, 1878, a mass of semiliquid peat suddenly and unexpectedly started to move down the hill, cutting through the center of the little town. The peat, several feet thick and moving at some four to five miles an hour, engulfed everything in its way.

Drainage of the workings continued to be a serious problem and on a midwinter's night in June, 1886, a second slip occurred, this time with even more disastrous results. Two persons lost their lives and damage was done to property, including the Exchange Building, which was found to have its clock tower three feet out of perpendicular. The decision was taken subsequently to demolish the old building and in March, 1890, the foundation stone was laid for the present Christ Church Cathedral which, like its predecessor, dominates the town. The main building was completed in 1892, but at that time it had no tower. A tower was constructed by Austrian stonemasons about 1902. Before the planned

The second peat slip in Stanley in 1886. A view of John Street covered by a mass of liquid peat.

steeple on top of the tower could be built, the men left the job, which is why the present construction has a rather unorthodox appearance, but a solid look which marries well with the surrounding township and landscape.

When Captain Parker Snow wrote his description of Stanley from aboard the vessel *Allen Gardiner*, he had as passengers four members of the Patagonian Missionary Society. The reason for their trip to the Islands goes back to 1844, when the founder, Commander Allen Gardiner, established the mission. Gardiner had spent much of his life attempting to establish missions among the natives of South America. In 1841 he had visited Port Louis with his family to see about setting up a base in the Falklands from which he might work among the natives of Tierra del Fuego. During this visit to Port Louis he had made one unsuccessful trip across to Patagonia and then returned to England to raise funds for a further attempt. In September, 1850, Gardiner set out once again for the wilds of Patagonia with a small number of volunteers and sufficient supplies for six months.

Although a determined man, Gardiner was met with one crisis after another. Important supplies were left aboard the *Ocean Queen* which had landed them at Banner Cove. The natives became threatening and they were forced to move further along the coast, leaving some of their supplies behind. A boat was lost, and the contents, having been salvaged once, were also lost when exceptional tides carried them away. Gardiner had arranged for more supplies to be delivered but, unknown to him, no ship could be found to deliver them. Eventually, after much delay, a chance meeting in Montevideo between Gardiner's agent, Lafone, and Captain Smyley, resulted in Smyley agreeing to take the provisions to Banner Cove. Finally, on October 21, 1851, Smyley sailed into Spaniard Harbor, some forty miles from Banner Cove, and found all but Gardiner and one other member of the mission party dead of starvation. Smyley had been unable to find Gardiner and his companion at Banner Cove. In January, 1852, Gardiner and his companion were discovered dead at this place by HMS *Dido,* which had been dispatched to look for the missing members of the mission. Gardiner's diary bore witness to the tragedy and also left instructions on how his work should be carried out. Gardiner instructed that a mission station be set up on one of the islands in the Falklands, that a suitable vessel capable of sailing between the Falkland Islands and Tierra del Fuego be purchased, and that members of the mission should learn the language of the Fuegian Indian tribes. The latter he considered was most important in order that friendly natives might be persuaded to go across to the Falklands to be taught by the mission.

The arrival in Stanley of the mission schooner named after its founder heralded the beginning of another attempt to work among the tribes of Tierra del Fuego.

Permission had been given by the British government for the society to establish their new station on one of the West Falkland islands. In February, 1855, the schooner *Allen Gardiner* and a small party of mission members arrived at Keppel Island, on the north side of West Falkland.

In the same way that Gardiner had been fraught with problems, so were the efforts of the new missionaries. Fuegian families, including Jemmy Button, who had been one of the four young Fuegians taken back to England by Captain FitzRoy of HMS *Beagle* about 1830, were brought over to Keppel Island in 1858. They were trained in gardening, reading, writing, and religion. But in the following year, when the "discontented families of Fuegians" were being returned to Tierra del Fuego, members of the mission and crew of the *Allen Gardiner* were attacked at Wulaia and, except for one member of the crew, all were killed.

With no news being received of the *Allen Gardiner*, once again Captain Smyley's assistance was requested. As he had some eight years before, Smyley returned with news of the tragedy. Besides the lone survivor of the massacre, Alfred Coles, Smyley brought back to the Falklands a family of

Fuegians who had pleaded with him that they be returned to the mission station at Keppel Island. The return of these Indians to Keppel had significant developments for the future of the mission. It was through these Fuegians belonging to the Yahgan tribe that Thomas Bridges, a member of the mission who worked at Keppel, was to become sufficiently well versed in their language to converse with the tribes. Bridges at that time was only nineteen years old. During his subsequent work among the Yahgans in Tierra del Fuego, he produced the famous Yamana-English Dictionary, containing 32,000 words of Yahgan language.

Some three years after the massacre, the new superintendent of the Keppel Mission Station, the Reverend Waite Hocking Stirling, accompanied by Thomas Bridges, set sail for Tierra del Fuego in order to attempt a meeting with the Indians. Through the ability of Bridges to speak with the Yahgans in their own tongue, the meeting was successful, and many of the Fuegians were eventually to visit and stay on Keppel Island. The station thrived and with the help of the Indians developed into an extremely productive farm which was to become self-supporting. The station continued until 1898, when the remaining Fuegians were moved to a new mission station on the South American mainland. The eventual future of Indian tribes like the Yahgans was a sad one. With the development of Patagonia by settlers, the Indians were exposed to disease and to the somewhat ruthless attitude of some pioneers. Many died of disease and others were exterminated, with the result that today no true Indians remain.

5. A HUNTING GROUND FOR WHALERS AND SEALERS

Perhaps half a mile from the rocks there was that unmistakable smell of guano, a strong musty smell I associated with the fur seal. Yet the rocks looked bare of any form of life. Nothing moved. Sea conditions were ideal for a landing, so we launched the small dinghy and I began to pull toward the rocks. For some distance my back was turned to the shore, but the sound of crashing water made me turn. Suddenly the rocks were alive with the dark brown forms of hundreds of seals: the rocks had in fact been covered with sleeping fur seals which blended in so well with the terrain that we had failed to see them at a distance. As I approached, dozens of animals were leaping into the sea but not as I feared to head away out to sea, but actually toward me. Within seconds the water about the small dinghy was boiling with fur seals as they porpoised in the water about the boat. Instead of fear, the animals were showing curiosity and I thought how easy it must have been for those early exploiters to take these animals. Or did they realize my visit was for reasons of study and would bring them no harm?

Three species of seals breed in the Islands: the southern sea lion, the Falkland fur seal, and the southern elephant seal, with the leopard seal being an occasional visitor. The sea lion is the most common, forming small breeding colonies on many of the offshore tussock islands and in more remote parts of the main island coasts. Although fish do form part of their diet, squid and octopus are the mainstay. It is not an uncommon sight to see these animals diving through beds of kelp and bringing this prey to the surface, where it is thrashed and broken into pieces before eating.

The fur seal is more selective in its choice of breeding ground, preferring formidable offshore rocks, ledges, or deep undercut cliffs and generally inaccessible positions on which to form herds which might number several thousand animals. Although this seal, now protected from hunters, is slowly regaining its position, the total population of the Falklands is still only about twenty thousand animals, restricted to a few parts of the Islands. In contrast to the feeding habits of other seals, the fur seal relies on smaller forms of marine life, lobster krill being perhaps the most important form. They feed normally at night. Observing these animals on their rookeries during this time, one will note a considerable exodus as large numbers move out to sea, returning only at dawn. During the breeding season, when pups are taking

A portrait of a young male fur seal with females and pups in the background.

milk from the cows, one can hear the amazing sounds of high-pitched calls of pups and answering females as they arrive back to feed their offspring.

Half a century ago the elephant seal was a rare sight in the Islands, having been almost exterminated years before when sealers hunted it for its oil. Now, year after year, populations of this large seal—male bulls attain the weight of three tons—are slowly increasing. This species is one of the "true" forms of seals. Unlike the sea lion and fur seal, which use fore and hind limbs and flippers to lift their bodies and walk, the elephant seal relies on its stomach muscles for its main movement over land. For this reason these seals normally haul out to breed on the more easily approachable shores of sand or shingle. Even on close approach by humans this rather inactive creature will do little more than roll its huge watery eyes or open its gaping mouth with leisured effort. But the impassivity of this creature and other wild-life—the only "natives" of the Islands—was to be their downfall when man arrived upon the scene.

At the time the French were establishing their little colony at Port Louis on East Falkland, Captain John Byron with his two vessels, HMS *Tamar* and HMS *Dolphin,* entered Port Egmont, on Saunders Island, West Falkland, on January 12, 1765. In one of his reports, Byron mentioned that the beaches of Saunders Island were crowded with fur seals. Two years later, when Port Egmont was settled, there was no mention of any sealing activities, but when the British withdrew from Port Egmont in 1774, both American and French sealers were around the Islands. It is probable that Captain Cook's publication of his discovery of large numbers of fur seals at South Georgia during his voyages of discovery in 1772–1775

Female elephant seal being inspected by curious rockhopper penguins.

led indirectly to the exploitation of seals in the Falklands. Many of the ships bound for South Georgia would have called at the Islands to provision or overwinter. Although the seal colonies in the Falklands would have been small compared with those at South Georgia, they were nevertheless worthy of exploitation. It is not recorded when the first seal skins were taken, but probably one of the earliest large cargoes was that of the sealing vessel *States* from Boston. She is recorded as having a cargo aboard of thirteen thousand skins when she sailed from the Falklands in 1784. By 1785 sealers were leaving British ports, the first to go south being vessels belonging to the Enderby Brothers of London. It is not clear whether they also called at the Falklands to seal, but it is known that in 1786 a British vessel was sealing at Saunders Island, selling skins to other vessels calling at the Falklands.

One of the most successful sealers was Edmund Fanning, a native of Stonington, Connecticut. He made several visits to the Falklands, his first being in 1792. His records illustrate a little of the sealing trends in the Islands, and many of the rookeries he described are known sites of fur seals today. In the year of his first visit he spoke of seals being seen in great numbers on some of the outer islands and recorded that he saw some forty ships, both American and British, procuring seals around the Islands. Fanning was specifically interested in fur seals but remarked that many of the vessels he saw were engaged in "elephanting," the taking of elephant seals for their oil. This particular industry was at this time reaching a peak and in the Falklands was

Beauchene Island where the American sealer Edmund Fanning recorded large numbers of fur seals.

to remain one of the most steady forms of sealing. During a subsequent visit to the Falklands in 1798, Edmund Fanning records that sealing was still in progress but not on the scale evident elsewhere in the Southern Hemisphere. On Masafuera Island, off the Chilean coast, it was reported that year that more than a million fur seal skins were taken. Some 1,797 sealers were engaged from fourteen ships, and three million skins were taken over a period of seven years. The pattern of destruction was the same at South Georgia, where by 1800 sealing became systematic and some 122,000 seals were killed in 1881.

Knowledge of our seal colonies today, coupled with the writings of past sealers like Fanning, do show that seal populations in the Falklands were small compared with those farther south. It is also evident that the Islands' fur seal rookeries were not as accessible, the animals choosing the bases of steep cliffs, offshore rocks, and largely unapproachable coasts on which to form their colonies. Except by the few, more determined, sealers, the animals were not as easily obtainable as their southern counterparts, which bred largely on open accessible beaches. During my studies of the Islands' seal population, I have concluded that it was this which actually saved the fur seals from extinction in the Falklands. One factor which was probably of even greater importance to the sealers and whalers of that day was the abundance of excellent harbors in the Falklands which could be used by their ships and crews for overwintering bases or as havens where they could repair and replenish their vessels for voyages farther south. Perhaps because they were farther away from the eye of authority, or perhaps because these hunters recognized that the west side of the archipelago was richer in wildlife, the majority of the bases were established on that side of the Islands. Places-like West Point Island (at one time known as Albatross Island), Grave Cove (still marked by a number of graves which date back to early sealing times), Beaver Island, named by the crew of the American ship *Beaver,* and New Island all became self-styled homes of American whaling and sealing vessels.

New Island was to become one of the most famous and originally got its name from those men sailing out of American ports such as New Bedford and New York. At New Island there is a small bay called Coffin's Harbor and just offshore an island which bears the same name, clearly dating from the time when the famous Quaker family of Coffins sailed out of Nantucket for the Falklands on whaling expeditions. At New Island the Americans kept a depot ship on which they stored barrels of penguin and albatross eggs taken from the colonies on this island. Pigs, and later rabbits, were introduced as a source of fresh meat, and "wild fowls" (upland geese) were always in plentiful supply. Undoubtedly one of the most vivid accounts of this island was that written by Captain Charles Barnard in a description of his "Sufferings and Adventures" during the years 1812–1816. After rescuing the survivors of a British merchant vessel, Barnard, American master of the brig *Nanina,* was marooned with four of his crew on New Island. For nearly two years, much of the time on his own, for even his companions deserted him, Barnard lived on the island surviving on what he could. In search of fur seals, the skins of which these men needed for clothing, Barnard in his narrative describes vividly the task involved in obtaining the skins and gives us an insight into the type of men who ventured south to seal.

The dry-stone building constructed by Captain Barnard in 1812 on New Island.

On the 25th we went down a steep gully, formed by a wide rent in the rocks, extending from the tops of the cliffs, and leading through to the sea, in quest for fur seals and their pups; we descended to the sea, and clambered along the rocks towards the place where we had seen the seals in great abundance; but though we were near to them, we were prevented from going any further by the sea rolling under the cliffs, the bases of which, by the continual action of the sea, had been hollowed out and formed into deep caverns. To effect a passage

84

over this place, Louder, who was a good swimmer, took one end of a rope, and swam with it to the other side, where he was followed by Green. We on this side fastened Ansel, who could not swim, to the middle of the rope, and lowered him away, while those on the other side hauled him over, without his even touching the water, which was very cold. I then swam across, leaving Albrook to send our knives, steels, clubs, and clothes across, by securing them to the middle of the line, which we drew over. There we found a large number of seals, which were very tame, and easy to kill; probably they

West side of New Island where Barnard hunted fur seal.

had never been visited or disturbed by man, in this almost inaccessible retreat. We took about one hundred and twenty, mostly pups, and remained all night, which we passed most uncomfortably on the rocks, in this cold and exposed situation.

We finished skinning the seals, and carried them to the hauling place, and by means of the rope and the man on the other side, got them safely across this dangerous current. We waited for a smooth time before we crossed, and then two of us plunged into the water, among a great many seals, who were playing and jumping about in the briny flood. The one who remained with Ansel, lowered him, while we hauled him over. After all were across, we carried the skins to the foot of the ravine, and left them there: we ascended to the top, and then proceeded to our residence, distant about one mile. We immediately prepared something to eat, and then retired to rest; both of which we absolutely needed.

We went for the skins the following morning. When we arrived at the cliffs, we attached one end of the rope to a stake, and carried the other down with us as far as it would reach, to assist us in regaining the top with our burdens, which consisted of five or six skins for each. Having in this laborious manner conveyed all the skins to the top, the severest part of the labour was yet to be completed. After a short intermission we resumed our task, and carried the skins to the place denominated our home, and placed them all in a pile. I then directed that all should stand round it, and that each man should draw a skin in rotation, and put it to what use he thought proper, which would prevent all disputes in washing and drying them. This mode of distribution I established as a general rule, and it was cheerfully agreed to by the others.

Besides the wild geese, the eggs of penguins and albatrosses, wild berries, and the cattle they hunted on the main islands of East and West Falkland, the sealers and whalers relied on pigs as a source of fresh meat. Pigs were turned loose, especially on the smaller tussock-grass islands where they were found to thrive. Left to multiply and unattended, the pigs decimated many of these small tussock islands. In some cases the hunters would deliberately set fire to the tussock grass in order to drive the semiwild hogs out of their dense cover. Many islands never recovered and even today evidence remains of early overgrazing and fire. Although they are not easy to locate, in my own wanderings about many of the more remote islands in search of wildlife, I have come across the remains of sealers' encampments. A few strategically placed stones or rocks, where a long boat would have been turned over and placed to form a shelter might be the only clue, but if one was fortunate an odd bottle could be unearthed. My best find has been the remains of a sealing lance and a leather moccasin preserved beneath a thin layer of peat.

No account relating to the early sealing activities in the Falkland Islands would be complete without full mention of William Horton Smyley, born in Rhode Island in 1792. Smyley made his first appearance in South American regions at the age of sixteen or seventeen and even at an early age had a distinctive career under Admiral Brown of the Argentine Navy. In the 1820s he was sealing in the South Shetlands, establishing himself in the Falklands about 1830. At this time, with a group of runaway seamen and a shallop built from an old wreck, he commenced a business of sealing and cattle-hunting, selling his spoils to other sealing and whaling vessels. So notorious did he become for killing beef that he acquired the nickname of "Fat Jack of the Bone House." By 1832 Smyley owned a fine American schooner, the *Saucy Jack,* which he used for illicit sealing. His reputation as a rogue and even a pirate grew, but he also became known for his daring, courage, and humanity to others, and records exist today showing the number of shipwrecked men he saved. (Several of his rescue missions were recounted in the previous chapter.)

In 1839, Lieutenant Robinson, a naval superintendent, reported that Smyley represented himself as an officer in the United States services and an employee of the American government. Although the position was self-styled, it did not deter Smyley from his illegal operations and in that same year he was warned that Britain held exclusive rights to all fisheries around the Islands, and he was forbidden to return. However, Smyley continued his activities about the Falklands and farther south, authority often ignoring his sealing, probably because of the large numbers of lives he continued to save. For some years Smyley assumed authority of the seas about the Falklands, and even his own countrymen were at times subjected to his unorthodox methods. In 1846 the magistrate, Moore, reported how Smyley, on discovering an

Breeding group of sea lions. The males are identified by their heavier heads and thick manes.

88

American schooner lying off a seal rookery, donned the uniform of a lieutenant in the British navy, threatened the master of the schooner that he would sink the vessel unless he left, Smyley adding that the British government did not allow foreigners to seal about the Falklands. Upon this the sealers departed, leaving Smyley with a rich booty of seal skins.

During Smyley's operations about the Islands he owned a number of schooners, often large, well manned, and armed. About 1845, Governor Moody reported on a new vessel of Smyley's, the *Catherine*. This was armed with two cannons on carriages which he would fire when leaving Stanley Harbor, often causing some consternation to the inhabitants. Moody wrote: "I looked at his Register and Papers and found he was privileged to carry two guns and I was given to understand he fired them by way of a salute to me, for whom he professes to entertain a high respect." Moody was, however, somewhat concerned about Smyley's political activities and, when in 1845 there was a possibility of war between the English and French governments and the Argentine Republic, Moody reported of Smyley's friendship with General Rosas, Argentine president. He was concerned that Smyley, being "an active, bold, adventurous man with very few scruples in his various pursuits," might, with little encouragement from the Argentine government, undertake some daring exploit such as stealing the Military Chest, which held important government documents.

By 1847 Smyley was the owner of the schooners *Alonzo* and *America* and his commercial interests in Stanley increased. By 1850 his self-declared position as United States commercial agent for the Falkland Islands was approved by the United States president. Having an intimate knowledge of the sea channels about Tierra del Fuego, and with his amazing ability to speak Fuegian, he searched for the mission schooner *Allen Gardiner* in 1860 and discovered the massacre of the mission members. Later he saved and brought back the schooner to the Falklands. In 1861 he was appointed United States consul in the Falklands, and this was subsequently recognized both by the British government and the government of the Island. Smyley's last vessel was the 178-ton *Kate Sergeant*, which made its first appearance in Port Stanley about 1867. This vessel also had its own cannons and was probably the finest of his schooners. In 1868, at age seventy-six, Smyley was still commanding the vessel, but three years later, while on a visit to Montevideo, he contracted cholera and died. Rather sadly, there is no memorial to this unique character, although his house in Stanley still remains.

Whaling and sealing were very much an integrated business in the Falklands and it is difficult to determine from available records exactly what some ships and their crews were taking. Oil was the all-important product and when whales were not easy to find, the hunters would often supplement their cargoes with elephant seal oil. At New Island, Beaver Island, and West Point, receiving ships of between 150 and 400 tons might lie for many months, while the actual whaling would be carried out by tender vessels. On New Island today there still exist the remains of a small lookout point on one of the high cliffs. Here whalers would post a lookout watching for the telltale blow of a whale offshore. The whales were known to follow certain routes between the Islands or come into certain sheltered bays to calf. Once

Although whaling ceased in the Falklands at the turn of the century, many islanders saw service with whaling fleets farther south.

a sighting was made, a tender would be dispatched from her receiving ship to hunt the whale. The southern right whale was the main quarry about the Falklands, although sperm whales were probably the more important species hunted farther north.

Although the Falklands are associated with whaling, this was never a major area for the business. As early as 1854, a whaler which had been at New Island for eight months reported that it had only caught one whale in that time. In much the same way as the fur sealing developed, much richer whaling grounds were to be found farther south and in the Pacific. The Falklands were largely left as a place of replenishment and convenience, where seals and whales were taken to complete cargoes taken elsewhere.

The Falklands do, however, have the distinction of having had the first land-based whaling station in the Southern Hemisphere. Set up at New Island in 1908 by Salvesen & Co., of Leith, Scotland, it had only three catchers. The annual catch, mainly of sei and fin whales, was never to exceed seven thousand barrels of oil, and in 1916 the station was closed and moved to South Georgia.

Less than twenty years ago whales were not uncommon in Falkland Island waters. In certain areas where migrating whales had to pass through narrow channels in the archipelago, their blowing could be heard clearly on calm nights as they made their passage. Then quite suddenly, in the space of a few years, as whaling fleets depleted the larger stocks farther south and thus found it economical to take relatively smaller populations from areas such as the Falklands, the whales disappeared. Now the one-time common sperm, sei, fin, and rorquals are rare sights. The only true marine mammals commonly seen about our shores today are pilot whales, Peale's porpoises, Commerson's dolphins, and the much larger and predatory form of dolphin, the killer whales.

The first attempts at taking penguin oil in the Falklands are generally attributed to American sealers and whalers in the 1820s, but as was customary with these early exploiters, there are few records to indicate the extent of this particular form of oiling. In South Georgia, elephant seal hunters found the vast rookeries of penguins, probably those of king and

Left: Rockhopper penguins coming ashore. In such areas penguin oilers built corrals into which the birds were herded.

Below: King penguins on East Falkland. This species has always been rare in the Islands.

A penguin oilers try-pot and remains of an old encampment in the Islands.

macaroni penguins, both an alternative source of oil and a useful means of firing their try-pots with the skins of penguins. Records indicate that some 500,000 to 700,000 birds were taken annually on South Georgia, but it is very doubtful if the same numbers were reached in the Falklands.

The height of the penguin oil industry in the Falklands was reached in 1864 with seven vessels engaged in this work.

Many penguin rookeries, particularly rockhoppers, were destroyed. Taking advantage of the nature of these penguins to follow pathways from the sea to their colonies, stone corrals were built to intercept the birds, so that they walked into the corrals themselves. Here they were clubbed and then boiled down in large iron try-pots.

From 1864 to 1866 it is recorded that some 63,000 gallons of penguin oil were brought into Stanley. Those engaged in the industry generally accepted that eight rockhopper penguins produced one gallon of oil, so probably some half million birds were killed during this period. Unlike sealing, there were no regulations governing the industry until 1866 when the killing of penguins was prohibited on East Falkland, except by permission. West Falkland remained unprotected. Even so, the law was not brought into effect for the benefit of the birds, but simply to license the operation so that the government could levy a tax of £10 per eight thousand gallons of oil taken from penguins on Crown Land.

Fortunately the industry was only in operation for some sixteen years in the Islands, its decline being attributed to the war in France in 1871. Most of the oil had been exported to France where it was used in the fine leather trade.

How many birds were destroyed is not known, for the oilers had little interest in keeping records of such things. But from the total amount of oil recorded as shipped through Port Stanley, some 1.75 million birds must have been required. It is probable that more than 2 million penguins were killed during the years of operation.

6. DEVELOPMENT OF THE ISLANDS' PASTURES

Flying over the two main islands of East and West Falkland, one has the impression of a landscape dominated by gray-ridged hills. Low valleys intersect the hills, the valleys themselves often being divided by giant screelike formations known as *stone runs*, which sweep down from an apparent source on the high ridges. To explain these unique formations one must go back in time millions of years when the Islands were experiencing periods of freezing and thawing. This weathering acted on the layers of hard and soft quartzite sandstone, the softer layers being broken down into a fine mudlike substance on which the harder pieces slowly slipped and moved down from the higher ridges. The process took millions of years, but it is still extraordinary that rocks, some many tons in weight, were moved over areas of square miles.

Most of the Falkland Islands are composed of sedimentary rocks formed in the Paleozoic and Mesozoic periods (600–270 million and 225–135 million years ago). There is little evidence of volcanic rock in the Islands.

Although the Falklands lie close to the continent of South America, geologists believe that the Islands were at one time part of South Africa. Fossils, silicified wood, and the way the rocks have been formed here are all very similar to those of the Barakar Beds in India and the Ecca Series of South Africa—all adding evidence to the theory of continental drift

The main islands of East and West Falkland—a terrain of gray-ridged hills with low valleys intersected with screelike formations known as stone runs.

and the belief that the Falkland Islands formed the missing section of the Karroo Basin of Natal and Eastern Cape Province of South Africa.

The vegetation of the Falkland Islands might be described as tundralike. Although this description is not fitting to all regions, it could be applied to the main islands where coarse grasses, ferns, low ground-hugging shrubs, and sedges grow on predominantly peaty soil. Again from a flight position perhaps two or three thousand feet above the archipelago, one can pick out the different pattern growths. The most noticeable are the large areas of light, buff-colored white grass (*Cortaderia pilosa*) with darker patches of deep green, scattered at random over this lighter backdrop. Forming the next most dominant growth is the shrub diddle-dee (*Empetrum rubrum*), while other plants add an array of different shades—from the deep reddy-browns of some ferns to rich yellows and greens of fine grasses, mosses, and sedges.

When the Islands were first discovered, the few early naturalists who reported on the vegetation spoke at length about the discovery of a giant grass which grew on the smaller offshore islands in the archipelago and on some areas of the coasts of the main islands. Few reported in detail about the vegetation of the inland regions. However, the indication is that growth was generally much lusher than it is today, for there are accounts of riders journeying through areas of grass and wild celery which reached their stirrups. Such areas are unknown today.

When de Bougainville landed at Port Louis to establish his little settlement, he brought with him seven heifers and two bulls. These were to be the basis of one of the finest herds of cattle in the Southern Hemisphere, although from time to time other settlers brought animals to the Islands. The cattle were allowed to roam and, largely unattended, multiplied rapidly on the rich pastures of East Falkland. In 1838 when HMS *Arrow* surveyed that island, the first officer, Lauchlan Bellingham Mackinnon, reported that about thirty thousand head of fine cattle roamed the land. The year before this report, Captain George Grey of HMS *Cleopatra* reported seeing at San Carlos (on the opposite side of East Falkland to Port Louis) fourteen or fifteen separate herds numbering some forty animals each, "evidently increasing, from the number of calves in every flock." Grey calculated that the wild cattle then numbered some twenty thousand, and also reported that some four thousand wild horses roamed the island, as did herds of pigs.

Until 1839 the cattle were restricted to East Falkland, but in that year Captain Bartholomew James Sulivan, then senior commander of Her Majesty's vessels in the South Atlantic, directed that cattle should be introduced into West Falkland as well. Eleven bulls and fifty-five cows were landed at White Rock Bay, in the north of that island. Eighteen years later, Governor Thomas Edward Laws Moore reported that the herds numbered between two and three thousand head.

The potential value of the increasing herds was probably first recognized about 1823, when the government of the United Provinces of the River Plate (Argentina) offered fishing and cattle rights to Louis Vernet. Between 1826 and 1831 Vernet established some ninety settlers at Port Louis, who were largely engaged in the processing of dried fish, dried meat (then known as jacked beef), and cattle hides, which Vernet sold in South America.

About 50 percent of the land area in the south of East Falkland is an undulating region which rarely rises more than one hundred feet above sea level. It probably qualifies as the only plain in the Falklands. This area, known as Lafonia, is covered largely with white grass.

Samuel Fisher Lafone, a merchant of Montevideo, Uruguay, first became interested in the Falkland Islands late in 1843. A report by Moody concerning large numbers of cattle and horses that then existed on East Falkland and the need to exploit them by a soundly financed company prompted Lafone to look into the project. Early in 1844, Mr. Martinez, agent for Lafone, visited the Islands to investigate the possibilities of such a venture. In March, 1844, Lafone made his proposals. His hopes were to purchase all the land to the south of Wickham Heights on East Falkland, thus availing himself of over half the area of that island. This was refused by Moody, and Lafone was offered the land lying to the south of the isthmus at Darwin Harbor, the area known now as Lafonia. Lafone planned to establish his own settlement in this area, spoke of his intentions to send down a clergyman and a prefabricated church, and to establish some form of education for the children of his settlers. These, he proposed, would be made up of five-ninths from the Shetland Islands, one-ninth of men from the River Plate for the management of cattle, two-ninths from Chile, and the remainder would be what he termed "intelligent Basques" to erect buildings, etc. Lafone also proposed to import some twenty thousand sheep over a period of four years and three thousand tame cows for use by the settlers. Lafone's contract was signed in London on March 16, 1846. For the land he was to pay £60,000 in installments. In addition, Lafone was to have complete charge of all wild stock on East Falkland—cattle, horses, goats, and swine—with the provision that Lafone at the end of his contract would have established a grand total of twenty thousand head of cattle, horses, mares and geldings on the entire East Falkland. This figure seems to contradict earlier estimations of cattle and horses already existing on the island.

Lafone almost immediately ran into difficulties. Montevideo, where he lived, was under siege and he was prevented from commencing operations until the midwinter of 1847. At that time his manager, Williams, arrived at Port Louis aboard a Norwegian vessel, *Napoleon,* with horses, supplies, and 102 men. More problems were encountered when it was discovered that the area purchased by Lafone was smaller than originally estimated. Concessions had to be made and the whole question was not resolved until a new agreement was drawn up in January, 1850. Lafone himself, who could not speak English, never visited the Falklands, so all his business was carried out through Williams who, Governor Rennie reported bitterly, continually obstructed intending pioneers.

Lafone's agreement to supply beef and cattle to settlers and government was a continual source of dispute. Supplies were neither regular nor sufficient, and the cattle driven to Stanley by Williams' gauchos were often so wild they could not be handled by the settlers and therefore reverted to Lafone's control. By 1849 Lafone had become heavily in debt to a company of merchants in the city of London who had financed his venture. In 1851, his brother, Alexander Ross Lafone, issued a prospectus of the "Royal Falkland Land, Cattle, Seal and Whale Fishery Company" in a bid to sell shares in Lafone's operation in the Falklands. That same year a committee met in London to form a company with a view to buying Lafone's rights and interests in the Islands. On April 24, 1851, the first meeting of the newly formed Falkland Islands Company was held in the city of London. The company was incorporated and was granted Royal Charter by Queen Victoria on January 20, 1852.

Today Darwin Harbor and Goose Green settlement, a stone's throw apart, remains the largest outside of Stanley and the main farm of the Falkland Islands Company. Even though Lafone's plans did not succeed, his name survives on the plain of Lafonia, as do many of the old turf-built corrals used by his gauchos to herd cattle. Houses scattered over Lafonia, bearing such names as Dos Lomas, Tranquilidad, Ponchos Shanty, and Old Orqueta House, although now in ruins, also bear witness to his operation.

With Lafone's establishment there came a rapid decline in cattle herds on account of Williams embarking on whole-

The Falkland Islands Company farm at Darwin on the edge of the plain of Lafonia.

sale slaughter for hides and tallow. Across the narrow isthmus which divides the southern part of East Falkland from the north, Williams' gauchos built a turf wall (still visible today although now topped with gorse bushes). This prevented those cattle on the great plain to the south from escaping from the gauchos. To the north the cattle were ruthlessly hunted, not only by these men but also by sealers and whalers and by the settlers themselves. In 1860, the government resumed ownership of the wild cattle and issued a notice to the effect that people would be fined for taking the animals. In 1847, it was estimated that there were some eighty thousand cattle, although it is doubtful if an exact number was known. The only real survey was made by the surveyor general in 1859, when 6,611 cattle were counted on the whole of East Falkland.

Cattle killing occurred principally in the summer months when small groups of gauchos on horseback would move from area to area, usually within sight of the coasts where the best cattle were generally found. The men rode together until a herd was sighted and then, approaching as close as possible without being detected by the cattle, each man would ride swiftly into the herd to lasso a selected animal. One end of the lasso would be fastened to the *cincha* or girth of the saddle, the other thrown as a noose about the animal's neck. Throwing the animal, the gaucho quickly dismounted, while his horse kept a strain on the lasso. Approaching the animal from behind, the gaucho would then cut a sinew or tendon behind the foreshoulder—a cruel practice and one that left the animal helpless. This "cutting down" would continue throughout the day, the gauchos retracing their steps the following day to kill and skin their catch. Moody wrote that

A Falkland shepherd. The handmade horse gear follows a design of that used by gauchos when they came from South America to work the Islands' cattle.

cattle hunting in the Falklands was very different from that practiced in Argentina, where the climate was milder and the ground of the pampas was firm. In the Falklands the gauchos had to contend not only with a heavier and wilder animal but often with severe climatic conditions. Of the gaucho Moody wrote:

> It is a life of delightful excitement and of skill and courage in which they may well be proved. The only repose after a day of great bodily exertion is on the bare ground, their saddle gear serving for bed and pillow and their poncho, with the addition of a rug or blanket, or perhaps a strip of painted canvas if the day's work ends near a corral, to shelter them from every inclemency of the weather.

Moody's words were to come back to me one day as I journeyed across an area of East Falkland. I had stopped for a night's rest overlooking a remote piece of coastline. The position I had chosen was a small but sheltered depression on a gentle slope facing north, therefore taking advantage of the sun's warmth. On a plateau at the top of the slope I had discovered the remains of a turf corral, now no more than a slightly circular grass-covered mound above the normal level of the surrounding ground. As I settled down to camp I could well imagine the hardships which those men endured, often a cool wind and the threat of rain showers to add to a cramped body after a day's exertions. On the credit side, however, there is the very peace of such places with only the nearby sea and the sounds of wildlife to break the silence. While preparing myself a meal, I wondered how the gauchos had fared and quite suddenly the answer was there. Precisely where I had picked my camp site, cutting a square of turf under which I proposed to bury my rubbish, I came across a layer of ash. Probing deeper I found the remains of some beef bones and, then to my utter delight and surprise, not just one but a number of old handblown wine bottles! These were later identified as being of a type made in the period when gauchos would have roamed these lands.

No records exist to indicate the original breed of the Falkland cattle, but it is known that they were long-haired, had broad forelimbs and small hindquarters, and large spreading horns. Some homes still display sets of these horns, which are reputed to have been taken when the cattle roamed wild. Today a small herd bearing these distinctive features and resembling closely the Spanish fighting breeds remains on an almost enclosed peninsula at Volunteer Point, on East Falkland. Being within a short distance of Port Louis, on land which has been under the same ownership since the days of cattle hunting, it is quite possible that these animals are direct descendants of those original herds. When crossing the Camp today one sees few cattle, and surprisingly the sheep, which number over 600,000 and form the Falklands only industry of wool production, are not always evident.

While the wild cattle were being decimated, sheep were already on the increase. Although a few sheep had probably been brought to the Islands before Whitington's arrival in 1840, it is generally accepted that the first main attempt at sheep raising was by this colonist. Whitington brought with him thirteen sheep and four studs. A year later a Mr. P. Sheridan, an English subject living in Buenos Aires who had been raising sheep for a number of years in Argentina, presented Moody with a gift of twelve animals. At first the attempts at raising sheep were not altogether successful. Moore, the magistrate, viewed the efforts at sheep raising a failure, reporting to London that there were no shepherds to watch the sheep. Rams were allowed to remain with the ewes at all times, resulting in lambs being born in the more severe months. In 1846, he reported that of the nine hundred sheep so far imported only one hundred remained, and only two bales of wool had been exported. Moody, on the other hand, believed that "all these things of course will be altered when sheep farming is adopted by persons proposing to make it their livelihood."

Undaunted by the earlier setbacks, Moody continued his campaign for making the Falklands into an agricultural colony. In 1847, he proposed that seven farms should be set up in the Islands and run by farming families from Britain. Each family would receive assistance from the British government and would be supplied with horses, ploughs, and stores. Moody's plan, however, was not to materialize, probably being discarded in favor of Lafone's proposals, which were being negotiated with London at the time. At the same period as Moody made his suggestion, one Captain R.C. Packe took a lease on East Falkland and shortly afterwards imported a number of sheep, along with a trained shepherd— probably the first in the Islands.

Most sheep were at that time being brought from South America and were therefore not adapted to the climate of the Falklands. Smaller numbers of pure bred, hardier animals came from England and eventually these were to form the basis of the Islands' flocks. By 1859, there were nearly eight thousand sheep in the colony, composed mainly of Cheviot

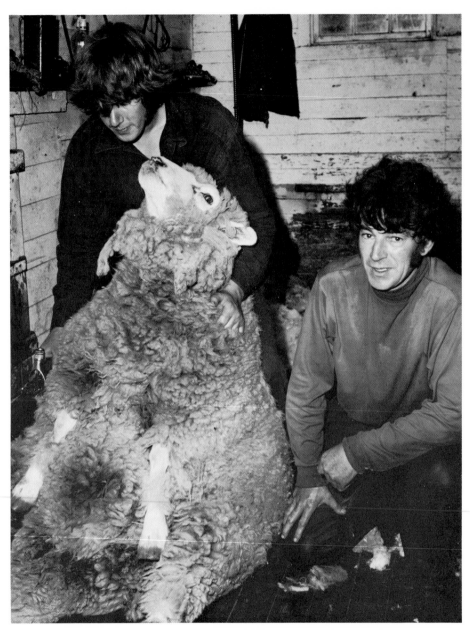

A large sheep, which could yield a fleece of some fourteen pounds.
Average weight for the Islands is about eight and a half pounds.

and Southdown breeds. Sheep did well on the pastures, car-
casses sent into Stanley for marketing averaging sixty-five
pounds in weight and fleeces often attaining ten to eleven
pounds, with an average of nine pounds. Today production
is on the average slightly lower which, with a generally better
class of stock, indicates that pastures have decreased in qual-
ity. It was not until 1867 that sheep farming spread to the
West Falkland mainland when a Wiltshire farmer James L.
Waldron and Edward Packe, a brother to Captain R.C. Packe,
took leases on land at Port Howard and Many Branch Harbor
respectively. Waldron, having chartered a barque, the *Diana*,
carried all his requirements from England. He brought Ex-
moor sheep and also a number of Merino. Wooden sectional
buildings originally built for the Crimean War were also
imported, some of which remain at Port Howard today. A
year later it was reported that all available land on the West
Falkland mainland had also been taken.

Those settlers moving to West Falkland found a surprisingly different terrain to that on East Falkland: the area was
far more hilly, with the east coast generally lacking the low-
lying beaches seen on the eastern and southern coasts of
East Falkland. On the east coast they found several excellent
harbors, almost landlocked. Port Howard was one of these,
which Waldron had been quick to appreciate when he looked
at the area. To the south, the island is broken into a maze
of inlets, channels, and bays, often with formidable cliffs,
stacks or high, detached rocks, and bluffs. To the southwest
of West Falkland, the mainland breaks away to form a com-
plex of islands such as Weddell, Beaver, and New Island,
among which lie many other smaller islands, islets, and stacks.
Generally the west coast of West Falkland does not have

the high elevations of the east and south. To the northwest, Byron Heights near the coast forms another impressive array of sheer cliffs broken only by small bays. From this point on the mainland, with intriguing names such as Death's Head and Grave Cove, the archipelago sweeps out northwest with a group of islands such as West Point, Carcass, Gibraltar Rock, South Fur, and the Jason Islands. Finally to the north of West Falkland the coast is broken into a mass of some fifty islands, islets, and reefs. To the outer extremity are islands like Keppel Island, Saunders (where the first British

A small sheep farm unit on Carcass Island in the northwest of the Falklands.

settlement was established at Port Egmont), and Pebble Island. These three larger islands all have fairly high elevations, while the mass of smaller islands which they embrace, strangely, are very flat and low lying, as are the north shores of West Falkland.

Sheep farming in the Islands increased rapidly and between the years 1871–1875 over 2 million pounds of wool were exported. With the demand for wool due to the Franco-Prussian War, prices rose to a record one shilling and sixpence (27 cents at that time) per pound. Up until that time wool from the Falklands had been sold as River Plate wool and was undistinguishable from that imported from Argentina. About 1873, it appeared on the British markets as Falkland wool and in 1874 the occupation of the Falkland Islands was described officially as "sheep farming," the number of sheep given as 170,000. By 1898, the official Stock Returns gave a total figure of 807,211 sheep—the highest sheep population ever recorded for the Islands. Sheep farming is directed entirely at the production of wool, with meat as a by-product used for local consumption only. Sheep are raised on slightly varying systems of large-scale ranching, depending on the size of the farm. On the East and West Falkland mainlands the farms are large, with the Falkland Islands Company (FIC) holding the largest area of land. Today that area is in the region of 43 percent of the total land in the Falkland Islands. Apart from this holding, an additional fourteen estates farm the remaining land on these two main islands. In the past few years, however, there has been a call for land division and the establishment of more smaller, owner-farmed units to replace company-owned estates. This has resulted in a small section of FIC land being sold for subdivision and subsequently three other estates being divided. Thus there are now over a dozen additional separate farm units on the mainlands.

As soon as all available land had been taken on the two main islands, by 1868, attention was given to the larger offshore islands which make up the archipelago. Farms were established on these too and today there are nine units operated either by small companies or run and owned by single family concerns.

Farms in the Falklands practice little agriculture, since it is not the general practice to grow crops of any kind. Work on the sheep farms generally begins in the spring month of

Above: Moving wool by small craft at West Point Island. Until the 1970s the small island farm relied heavily on small vessels for moving supplies.

Right: Handshearing, a practice which came to an end in the late 1960s when this picture was taken.

Rolling a fleece after shearing, still an important operation on any farm.

October with lambing. Later in November the younger sheep, hoggets (twelve to thirteen months old), are shorn first, followed by the older sheep. Final shearing is on the ewes, depending on the season's progress, usually between January and February, which is the Islands' late summer season. In March the sheep are dipped, or plunged into a container filled with disinfectant to remove any parasites. This practice is being discontinued to a large extent because of the absence of parasites. The sheep then are returned to their paddocks for the winter. During the winter months—May through August—work is concerned mainly with care and maintenance of the farm equipment and facilities.

For those pioneers establishing the early farms, whatever the size, it was an arduous task ridden with frustrations. Many of the basic needs had to be imported, such as timber for building, as well as basic food requirements like flour, sugar, etc. The need for immediate shelter in the unpredictable climate of the Falklands dictated to a very large extent the type of building which was erected and which, perhaps by tradition, continues today. Many of the early farmers saw the advantage of bringing small prefabricated wooden buildings with them. Basic shelter was quickly available and then, as time and progress permitted, these buildings were added to. Strangely, in a country where there is a natural predominance of stone, little was used for building and today stone cottages and buildings are not common in Stanley or the Camp.

Imports were expensive, so the tendency developed for design of a very fundamental, practical form rather than of any architectural merit. Early pioneers often clad their houses with timber shingles but, perhaps due to the extra costs of shipping or the increased time needed to put them on a building, these were soon replaced with corrugated iron sheeting, another feature of many buildings today which the visitor must find rather unique. Partly due to the expense involved in shipping, but often because supplies could not be obtained immediately, adaptations were made. Settlers were often experts at adapting themselves and their tools in order to overcome a particular requirement. Many a farm or house, especially in the Camp, still exhibits such adaptations, such as sheep pens and garden fences and even chairs

An island settlement house about 1890. The horses are carrying panniers of peat.

constructed from old oak barrel staves. Shipwrecks at one period were not uncommon around the Islands' shores and they became a most important commodity, not only supplying an array of items from their cargo but also the hulks of vessels being sought after for their timbers. Many houses and sheds still standing are constructed mainly from ships' timbers, while others sport the typical narrow doors of ships.

Although hardships were many for the early settlers setting up their homesteads and farms, living in a wild, hitherto untouched land had a very special attraction. Although life was simple in many respects, it was full in others. Making up for the lack of readily available provisions colonists quickly learned to adapt and make use of the natural environment around them. From the earlier sealers and whalers they had learned to use the eggs of penguins, albatrosses, and other wild birds for food. The wild upland goose was also known to be good eating. Fish were plentiful, as were other seafoods, and at certain times of the year wild berries were available for making jams and preserves. Almost unlimited amounts of meat from sheep and cattle were always available. Although the soil was predominantly peaty and could be burned as a fuel, the ground could also be tilled and with available fertilizers turned into excellent gardens. Even in these modern times, when the majority of Camp settlement houses have most modern conveniences and appliances that might be found in any town dwelling, one notes that living is still designed to an extent around the gardens, peat banks, the meat house, cows, and, although very much reduced these days, the exploitation of natural resources such as fish, wild birds' eggs, geese, and berries. In size the modern-day settlement has probably changed little from those that existed in the 1870s: the largest farm settlement, that of Darwin/ Goose Green, has a population of one hundred, next in size to the capital, Stanley, which has some nine hundred permanent residents. Other settlements vary in population down to the smallest which might be occupied by only one or two families.

7. THE GROWTH OF STANLEY

In 1847, Governor Moody wrote rather despondently of the large number of vessels that were seen each day passing the Islands, only a very few of which called into the new port of Stanley. The following year shipping around Cape Horn increased with the gold rush to California and the establishment of the Peruvian guano industry (seabird excrement which is used for fertilizer). Even so, the increase of shipping which called at Stanley for replenishment was minimal. Governor George Rennie, Moody's successor, felt that this was due to the lack of suitable charts and sailing directions. These were drawn up and published, with the result that in 1850 there was a substantial increase in the number of vessels—mainly passenger ships—which called at the colony.

Although the population did not exceed five hundred at that time, within six months Stanley saw a much larger number of ships' crews and passengers calling in. There was a demand for local produce and a market was set up selling fresh meat and vegetables to the vessels. In order to satisfy the requirement for fresh water, Rennie had a large reservoir built "lined with Italian terracotta tiles," and a special watering jetty. The reservoir remains today; the jetty has long gone, but its position is still marked by two sections of ships' masts sunk into the waterfront, which were used to tie up vessels taking on water.

With the general increase of shipping around the notorious Cape Horn, the number suffering from the stormy seas of that region also increased. Many "lame ducks"—ships that had lost their masts, rigging, or had been damaged in other ways—also called into the port. A new trade developed: ship repairing. The trade grew rapidly and by 1854 Rennie reported that wages were as much as 25 shillings, or six dollars per day. By 1867 the ship repair trade was at its height and, besides wages, merchants' prices soared. Unskilled labor was taken up by the new trade to such an extent that vegetables, although needed, were not produced. In a port where business depended on such casual trade there developed a tendency to charge maximum rates. Similarly, in a port where almost every item had to be imported at a high price, and where slipping and docking facilities were in short supply, damaged ships found that they often had to wait for long periods before they could be repaired. Gradually all these elements, in Governor Moore's words, were to give "an evil character" and the port was to lose many customers. Those ships that could maintain sail continued on past the Falklands to Montevideo, where repairs could be carried out much cheaper and quicker.

Another unfortunate factor which gave the Islands a bad name in the shipping world was what became loosely termed the "wrecking trade." Operated by the less scrupulous members of the community, this business probably developed as early as 1830. With no government control over wrecks until 1871, vessels and their contents used to be at the mercy of the finder. Often the masters and crews of these ships had to submit to what was in many cases open theft. For the unscrupulous it was an opportunity to make money; to those settlers with limited means, a wrecked cargo could often supply the necessities of life. Flour and grain were purchased

The wreck of the Leo Crespo on Swan Island about 1887. Such wrecks became an important commodity, not only supplying items from their cargo but timber from their hulks.

Port Stanley about 1890 with a number of sailing ships awaiting repair.

cheaply and luxuries otherwise unknown were suddenly available. The business was not restricted to the small operator and to the larger commercial concerns a wreck was of prime importance. Governor Rennie in 1851 described how an important commercial gentleman of Stanley approached him "in an unmistakeably sinister manner" regarding the wreck of a French vessel with a valuable cargo of silks and wines. The request was made for a few pounds out of the public chest so that he could make more purchases than his ready cash would allow. Often there was collusion between ships' crews and islanders, and ships were deliberately wrecked. Cargoes of liquor were prized and stories handed down over the years are still told by a winter fireside of how cargoes were taken from wrecks, then to vanish quickly into the Camp.

From about 1870, the ship repair trade went into its final decline. Steam vessels were replacing sail and as coal could be purchased in Punta Arenas, the southern port of Chile, very much cheaper than at Port Stanley, fewer vessels called in. During the gold rush and guano industry era, many unseaworthy vessels were pressed into service. The Cape Horn route was the final breaking point for many of these ships and to a large extent it was these which were forced to run for Port Stanley. Some of the vessels could be repaired and therefore meant trade for the colony, but many were condemned in the port and sold as hulks, never to leave Stanley again. Much of the final decline in the ship repair trade was attributed to Mr. Samuel Plimsoll, an English politician who promoted the Merchant Shipping Act of 1876. His agitation in Parliament compelled the British Board of Trade to make strict regulations about the seaworthiness of vessels before they were sent to sea by unscrupulous ship owners. Almost certainly this resulted in fewer ships foundering on the Cape Horn route, with the consequent decrease in trade for Port Stanley. Such was Mr. Plimsoll's achievement in this matter that ships today carry the "Plimsoll line," a register mark to ensure that they are not overloaded.

Sailing vessels continued to sail around the Horn and put into Stanley, but their numbers had shrunk considerably. Loss of trade and work resulted in many people leaving, some to Chile and others to the now growing sheep stations in the Camp. In 1873, the population numbered some eight hundred.

An all-important factor in the establishment of Stanley at its present site was the large amount of peat to be found in the area. Without peat as a fuel there could be no settlement, for there was no alternative form of fuel. The same applied to the establishment of the farm settlements in different parts of the Islands. The availability of a nearby peat supply was

Carting peat by sleigh in the 1800s.

to be the overriding factor in the selection of a site, even when there were seemingly better sites elsewhere. Just as important as the peat banks themselves, the cutting, drying, and carting home of the fuel were and are very important aspects of the islanders' lives. As soon as the spring commences with its drying winds, cutting also starts. The government still retains the post of a peat officer, whose job it is to allocate peat banks to households in Stanley and generally to ensure that certain rules of cutting are abided by. Although machine cutting has been tried on several occasions, mechanical methods have yet to be proven successful and peat is still cut by hand with a conventional spade. Today a lot of peat is cut by cutters working on contract, but it is still the responsibility of each household to arrange for the cutting of their particular peat bank each season. Peat replenishes itself but it takes a long time; once gone, one must go elsewhere. One peat bank, usually about 200 yards by 5 yards, can be dug to a depth of 6 feet. It will keep one household in fuel for fifty to sixty years.

Probably due to the fact that the Islands had no native human population and therefore the colony is still relatively young, traditions found in older communities are not prevalent. The few that do exist tend to show the nature of a life centered around a simple pattern, with little emphasis, for example, on the arts. There is no traditional dress, as one would find woolen ware in the Shetland Islands. Many islanders are artistic, but not enough time has passed to bring out a traditional piece of art. Only traditions connected with the gathering of food have evolved and many of these are

Carting peat from the banks after drying in stacks.

now dying. In any case, these are better termed customs. The annual collection of wild bird eggs, for instance—particularly of penguin and albatross eggs—developed into an important yearly event. Although not the case today, school children received an annual holiday of one day, November 9, to go "egging."

For the majority of people in Stanley, the egging season was usually marked by the arrival of local cutters, one-masted sailing vessels, bringing in large quantities of eggs from the outlying islands. One of my early experiences in the Islands was watching boxes of penguin eggs being brought ashore at the public jetty and being distributed to eager customers. Only a few hundred eggs were involved, but I knew that in earlier times many thousands of eggs had been sold from that same jetty. In those days it was not unusual for a vessel to arrive with its hold full; so great would be the weight of eggs that many layers at the bottom of the hold would be crushed or cracked. When these eggs were eventually reached, eager youngsters would descend to gather up what they could for free. Many penguin colonies close to Stanley were so extensively egged year after year that eventually, through lack of replacement birds, they vanished. Today the custom continues but on a diminished scale, and annual licenses are issued by the government to anybody wishing to collect eggs on payment of £1 per hundred eggs.

Around Christmastime, it being midsummer in the Falklands, another custom continued largely by people living in Camp settlements is the hunting of young upland geese. For many people in the Camp these young birds and lamb replace the more traditional turkey of the Northern Hemisphere. In the autumn months of March and April, many people still

Gentoo penguins at the start of egg laying. Many thousands of eggs were annually collected in earlier times.

collect wild berries and fruits, such as the wild strawberry, teaberry (*Myrteola nummularia*), and diddle-dee (*Empetrum rubrum*). The latter was often mentioned by early American sealers and whalers who first recognized it as similar to the red crowberry.

Although the custom of egging and berry picking may diminish over the years, the traditional Sports Week, usually held in Stanley at Christmastime and in the Camp after shearing is completed, will undoubtedly continue. Centered around horseracing, Sports Week is a popular event, with riders and their horses gathering at a meeting from all over the Islands. Organized race meetings started around 1875 at Goose Green, with the first official sports meeting in Stanley taking place in 1889. Races other than organized meetings were probably being run much earlier than these dates, especially in the Camp, where the horse was an important part of life.

Although some horses will probably always be retained for recreation, as a mode of transportation they are gradually being phased out on many farms. Motorbikes and Land Rovers are more popular and are even used extensively for sheep gathering. With no paved roads outside of Stanley, similar kinds of vehicles are needed to negotiate the simple forms of Camp track that link many of the settlements. Even then, a certain amount of driving skill and knowledge of the terrain are required. A good Camp driver learns to recognize the type of vegetation that grows on firmer ground and is certain to know from bitter experience that careless driving will result in his vehicle wheels breaking through the harder surface crust and into a soft mass of black peat. The danger of this occurring is so great that most vehicles traveling over the Camp automatically carry with them lengths of boarding and a lifting jack.

In the early days those people living on the West Falkland mainland and on islands relied entirely on the occasional visit by a small local schooner to receive their few supplies

Although farmers by profession, many islanders have developed skill in the handling of small boats, at one time the only means of communication among the islands.

The old Stanley town hall and post office. The cannon to the right of the building was used in days gone by to signal the arrival of mail ships.

and mail. For many, a visit to Stanley was a rare occurrence and many of the Camp womenfolk never saw Stanley at all.

Today the Islands have a small but well-established internal air service operated by the Falkland Islands government. As a result the people of the Islands must be some of the most air-minded people in the world. Established in 1948 using a small landplane, the benefits of such a service were very quickly realized. Soon after, two Beaver float aircraft were brought into use. With all settlements situated on harbors, float aircraft were better suited to the Islands, especially since the rugged terrain of most areas made the use of land aircraft difficult. A Beaver floatplane is still in service, but in 1979 the decision was made to try land aircraft again and

Falkland Islands Government Air Service Beaver float plane, above, operating
a service between Stanley and outlying settlements. Below: In 1979 a Brittain-
Norman Islander land aircraft was introduced by FIGAS.

a Brittain-Norman Islander was purchased. Although this landplane cannot serve all settlements, it has proved suitable for the type of operations the Islands require and now the floatplanes are being phased out.

The aircraft fly no regular route from their base in Stanley. According to bookings received for a particular day, they operate what might be termed short-haul flights between settlements, picking up and putting down passengers and freight. Although the average flight between settlements may only take twenty minutes or so, it is quite often that in the course of a day's flying the aircraft will circumnavigate the entire Falkland archipelago.

In many respects the air service in the Islands is very much a "bush" type operation. There are no navigational aids such as beacons or lights at the numerous field strips, and pilots rely on their knowledge of the landscape. For those who enjoy the thrill of flying in small aircraft, often at very low altitudes, one unique feature that may be experienced during a flight in the Falklands is that of "mail dropping." On the arrival of airmail into the colony, that which is destined for various Camp settlements is dropped to them from the air. Each settlement has its mail-dropping zone, marked with a large white cross on the ground. While making a low pass over this, the mail, securely fastened in a sandbag, is thrown out of the aircraft to a receiver below, who will have been advised by radio of the imminent drop.

Until 1971 the Falklands relied on shipping methods for passenger and mail communications with the outside world, the normal link being by a passenger-freight vessel that went between Stanley and Montevideo once a month. A freighter also traveled between London and Stanley four times a year.

In February, 1971, there began a regular external air link. This link, using an Albatross amphibian aircraft of the Argentine Navy, between Comodoro Rivadavia on the Argentine mainland and Stanley, was in itself an historical event. It was not only the beginning of air communications, but also communications with Argentina, which had not been known before. In November, 1972, this line of communication was taken a step further with the building of a temporary landing strip at Stanley and bringing into service a Fokker Friendship F27 aircraft operated by the Argentine Air Force. With once-weekly flights, the Islands were for the first time opened up to the would-be traveler. For those living in the Falklands, the sense of isolation started to diminish.

With the arrival of an external air service, the Islands were to receive regular airmail. Because of very close ties between the islanders and Great Britain, most mail received in the colony originated from the "mother country" and, prior to this air link, either came directly by ship from England, or was directed via Montevideo in Uruguay. Both these routes had a very long association with the history of mail service, going back to about 1852. At about this time, Smyley approached Governor Rennie and informed him that he was about to establish a commercial shipping link with Montevideo. He was planning on bringing the mails down about eight times a year, his voyages being regulated by the arrival and departure of the steamers to and from England. This Smyley was prepared to do for "£540 sterling per annum; this I believe is less than any Government vessel would cost." Rennie forwarded these proposals to the secretary of state, remarking that he knew of no other person "so well qualified for this undertaking." However, at about that time moves were being made in England to establish a regular mail service with the Islands, and when the Falkland Islands Company made known its intentions to establish a shipping link between London and Stanley, it was awarded the first mail contract. On July 1, 1852, the Company's first schooner, *Amelia,* arrived in Stanley. Traveling on board was the company's first colonial manager, John Dale, and also a mail contract worth £700. Thus the first "Mail Packet" service commenced between England and the colony.

Two years later the company found the mail contract disadvantageous and proposed to abandon it. Although this caused considerable concern and there were petitions to the Duke of Newcastle, the contract was abandoned and the mail service once again became irregular. In 1862 the Falkland Islands government acquired their own schooner, the *Foam,* and she made regular mail runs to Montevideo until 1873.

In 1880 a contract was signed with the Kosmos Steamship Company of Hamburg to carry mail. This was to be the first satisfactory regular service. Operating from Europe to Valparaiso, Chile, via the Straits of Magellan, her contract required her to call at Stanley once a month. This service was to run for twenty years. Similar services continued between Stanley and Montevideo, Uruguay, through to 1971 when the last regular sea link stopped with the withdrawal of the RMS *Darwin* and mail started to be flown in via Argentina. A sea link for mail direct between London and Stanley remained, and still continues today. Since the 1982 conflict with Argentina, airmail arrives by military transport aircraft via Ascension Island.

8. A DRAMATIC CHANGE

On the Argentine mainland coast lies the town of Comodoro Rivadavia, an oil town bearing the signs of a one-time boom, with its concrete office blocks, flats, and on its perimeter, shanty towns. Taking off from its modern-looking airport one gets an even better impression of the town amidst a land of bare red clay hills and small plains covered with sparse vegetation. In the summer, warm winds whip the eroded clay hills and envelope the town in dust; in winter the scene is changed to a sea of mud. Our flight path continued south along the coast so that one had a further impression of that particular part of Argentina—of vastness beneath a cloudless sky and still more rolling, rather arid-looking land. After following the coast for some hundred miles, the Fokker Friendship F27 turbo aircraft of Lineas Aereas del Estado (L.A.D.E., a civil airline operated by the Argentine Air Force) changed course and headed out over the South Atlantic. In less than two hours flying time, one approached a telltale pattern of cloud, like a great motionless umbrella. Protruding out from the edge of this "umbrella" one was presented with a new and different view of the Falkland Islands. Still mindful of the vast lands left behind, one was aware of the comparatively small size of the Islands. From our vantage point some 6,000 feet above, most of the archipelago was spread before us. Those passengers who were seeing the Islands for the first time would also marvel at the change and nature of the ground below as compared with the Argentine mainland. For myself, that November, 1972, was a strange experience. I was returning to the Islands, not as I had done so many times before, by ship, but by one of the first external flights and by a new line of communication with the outside world, through Argentina. As the aircraft descended over the north coast of East Falkland in preparation for its landing at Stanley, I was able to view the same landmarks I had seen when I first came to the Islands. Quite suddenly, I was looking at the Falklands from a completely different perspective. Landscape and landmarks, which in earlier passages had taken hours to come upon, view, and pass, were now passing beneath us in minutes, even seconds. The whole journey from our departure point on the mainland, at one time taking four or five days, had taken four or five hours. To me the Islands were no longer a remote and distant part of the South Atlantic. With a long sea voyage, changes were gradual and one could absorb the changing environment and accept more readily the change in language and culture; this had now gone.

In Comodoro Rivadavia I had studied fellow passengers.

A few islanders like myself were out of place: we were for-eigners with a different tongue and although facilities were there to help us, we were not at home. The remaining pas-sengers were Argentine, at ease in a home they knew. But landing at Stanley airport our Spanish-speaking visitors were the ones who suddenly found that they were out of place. Except for one or two L.A.D.E. personnel, everybody spoke to them in English, notices were in English. In the same way that I had met with contrasts when I first visited the Argentine mainland, our Argentine visitors showed amaze-ment at the differences in culture and life-style that they were now experiencing.

On August 5, 1971, in an attempt to settle the long-stand-ing dispute with Argentina over the sovereignty of the Is-lands, a Communications Agreement was signed between Britain and Argentina whereby access between the Falkland Islands and Argentina, hitherto restricted, would be opened up and improved. The establishment of this air link directly with the mainland in 1972 was the first step. Although the final question of sovereignty was not going to be resolved quickly, the direct link between the two countries and their peoples unquestionably lifted a cloud of uncertainty. For the first time in the history of the Islands, there was freedom of travel between the Falklands and Argentina. Islanders traveled over to the mainland and Argentines visited the Falklands and, as a result, an exercise of "getting to know one another" commenced. Direct telecommunications be-tween the Islands and the mainland were established, trade links began, and a number of basic commodities were shipped directly from Argentina. A fuel agreement was signed whereby gas, gasoline, and kerosene were imported from Argentina at a much reduced price than could be obtained by shipping such fuels from England. Children from the Falklands were offered scholarships in British schools in Argentina, and many took this opportunity to broaden their education and also to become bilingual. Unquestionably one of the major difficulties was the language barrier; the percentage of people from both Argentina and the Falklands who were bilingual was not high, so the average man-in-the-street had difficulty communicating. In an effort to overcome this problem in the long term, Argentine teachers qualified in both languages were brought over to the Islands to teach Spanish in the schools.

For nearly ten years the process of getting to know one another continued and few people would disagree that the exercise brought nothing but good. For many there developed a very close relationship between the two countries, friendships were made and still exist at all levels. There was talk of development between the two countries, probably in the fields of oil exploration and offshore fishing. However, there was still the overriding question of sovereignty and how best it might be resolved. Certainly no islander wished to take on Argentine nationality or wished to lose the close ties with the British mother country. Many Argentines who visited the Falklands and saw for themselves the nature and way of life of the islanders also acknowledged how difficult this would be. However strongly they might have felt what they had been taught was their right to the Islas Malvinas, many were sympathetic to the islanders' wish to remain British.

In November, 1980, a visit was made to the Falklands by the Honorable Nicholas Ridley M.P., minister of state at the Foreign and Commonwealth office, in order to speak to the islanders about ways in which the sovereignty dispute with Argentina might be resolved. The minister put forward three possible options: a condominium arrangement, a "freeze" on the question of sovereignty, and a lease-back arrangement with Argentina. The Islands' councils were asked to discuss these options with the people they represented and to report on their findings in preparation for Anglo-Argentine talks which were to be held in New York as part of a series of talks to try and settle the dispute. For many people, both Falkland islanders and Argentines, the dispute is very much an emotional one. Although the option of some form of lease-back arrangement was probably the only practical solution, it was not surprising that the legislature rejected the options other than the "freeze." The Argentine delegation at the New York meeting in turn rejected this proposal.

The feeling on that early morning of April 2, 1982, was one of utter disbelief as it suddenly became apparent to all of us in the Falklands that the Argentine naval fleet was heading for Port Stanley. Even in the final hour many felt that this was nothing more than a show of strength and, that having made a demonstration, the fleet would return to their bases in Argentina. This, as the world now knows, was not to be the case. As troops came ashore in heavily armored carriers, the islanders' disbelief turned to shocked amazement and restrained anger that such a small defenseless town, which had known nothing but peace, was being invaded. From that moment on, we were aware that the whole situation had changed dramatically; ten years of goodwill between two countries had been thrown away by one impatient thrust of a military regime.

For some seventy-two days we were to experience occu-

The conflict and surrender by Argentine forces in Stanley on June 14, 1982.

pation by foreign troops and military law, all of which has left a mark not easily erased. But the invasion by so many Argentine soldiers, many conscripted into the forces, was to reveal to these men that many things they had been taught about the Islands and the islanders were mythical. Numerous soldiers were to reveal to the islanders, like the peaceful invaders in the form of Argentine tourists had done in earlier years, that they were amazed to find, for instance, that people did not speak Spanish. Many expressed their dismay about invading such a small community, voiced their dislike of the military, and their main wish of returning to their own country.

Since the retaking of the Islands by the British Task Force, we have seen a new kind of invasion: of men, equipment, and supplies—a regrettable requirement needed to defend the Islands against further attack by Argentina.

Before the invasion there was much debate on what the future might have held for the Falkland Islands. Besides the sense of insecurity due in part to the sovereignty issue, the Islands were beset with economic problems. With an economy based mainly on the production of wool, the Islands' prosperity lay largely in the hands of a fluctuating world wool market. Due to these factors and the loss of the Islands' isolation, there was an element of unrest among the inhabitants. The Falklands by their very nature had always

Argentine Pucara aircraft lie destroyed on the outskirts of Stanley at the end of the conflict.

known a floating population, but the drift away from the Islands had increased. There were pleas for the steady emigration to be halted. It was suggested that diversification into other industries and the widening of opportunities for the young people who were leaving would halt the flow away.

In 1976 a report was published under the title "Economic Survey of the Falkland Islands." It followed a survey by members of the Economist Intelligence Unit, led by the Right Honorable Lord Shackleton, and the report was to be generally known as the Shackleton Report. It was an exacting and detailed work which left little unexamined, with terms of reference which covered not only economic development in the wool industry and forms of agriculture, but also development in the fields of oil, minerals, fisheries, alginates, which are extracted from seaweeds, and tourism. It also looked into such matters as social aspects and the need for improved installations and facilities. It was probably the first time that a study had been made of the social aspects, and on this subject the reporting team felt that dependence was a significant factor in the Islands' development. They reported that, although they found obvious qualities in the islanders, there was an apparent lack of enterprise at individual and community levels, with a "degree of acceptance of the status quo which verges on apathy." In the Camp they reported finding dependence of people on the companies and resident owners or managers in various respects and, although convenient and even comfortable in material forms, this did not encourage initiative. The team found signs of dissatisfaction with this situation, especially among the younger people, and felt that this attributed to the migration from the Camp. They also considered the fact that there had been little opportunity for individuals to acquire their own stake in the economy of the Islands, "most notably a stake in the land."

In an effort to alleviate this problem of dependence and to improve the opportunities for those acquiring a stake in the economy by obtaining land, the Falkland Islands Company agreed to sell one of their holdings, Green Patch. Some 72,000 acres was thus acquired by the Falkland Islands government and subdivided into six separate holdings. In 1980 they were leased to applicants with an option to apply for freehold possession after twenty years. Since the establishment of what was to be called The Green Patch Scheme, other large estates have been sold and subdivided into smaller units and taken up by individual islanders.

The Shackleton Report considered that there was a strong

Islanders raise a Union flag on an outlying island in the Falklands.

social need for a road network to link up some of the major settlements. In 1978, supported by a £1.157 million grant from the Ministry of Overseas Development, a major road project was started, the plan being initially to link Stanley with Darwin, the next largest township outside the capital. By 1983, although the conflict was to halt proceedings, only 12½ miles of an all-weather, unsurfaced road had been constructed. Now that a new airport is under construction at Mount Pleasant, a position between Stanley and Darwin, this road will be upgraded.

Between the Falkland Islands and the southern tip of South America there lie two of the last greatest unexplored oil basins in the world, The Magellan Austral Basin, which lies beneath much of the southern tip of Patagonia and Tierra del Fuego, and the Malvinas Basin, which lies beneath an area of sea situated between the Falkland Islands and the coast of Patagonia. In 1975 a United States Geological Survey bulletin estimated the oil reserves of these areas at some 200 billion barrels, nearly six times the estimated North Sea oil reserves. Other investigators have been more cautious, pointing out that it would take a number of years of exploratory drilling before estimates and field sizes could be made. The Shackleton Report concluded its findings on a nonoptimistic note with regard to the potential commercial gains for the Islands from any exploration. It also pointed out that there would be need for a much improved political climate with Argentina before any oil companies would be prepared to embark on any exploration program.

Probably one of the greatest prospects for development lies in the fisheries about the Falklands. For some years, Russian, Polish, German, and Japanese fishing fleets have been working in this region of the South Atlantic exploiting the rich fishing resources. Surveys carried out on a commercial basis indicate that two species, hake and blue whiting, are probably the most important, with a sustainable yield for whiting in the region of 1 million tons per year. Another fishing resource is the shrimplike crustacean krill. Throughout the zone south of the Antarctic Convergence, the Antarctic krill *Euphausia superba* is abundant. Antarctic Convergence is the name given to one of the great natural boundaries in the waters of the ocean, where the cold waters of the Antarctic meet the warmer subantarctic waters. This krill, which can attain a maximum length of sixty millimeters, occurs in dense swarms. When the great blue whales were prolific, they were estimated as taking some 175 million tons of krill per year as food. Various recent estimates of the sustainable yield range between some 50 million and 150 million tons per year. Approximately 16 percent of the body weight of krill is made up of a high-grade protein. It is expected one day that this will be commercially exploited as an additive for animal food and even for human consumption.

The Falklands' role in any fishing venture is still questionable, as modern fishing methods do not require shore-based processing plants. The Islands could, however, offer some services to such fleets and also sheltered harbor facilities for the transfer of catches and bunkering. This is currently happening with Polish fishing vessels using the Islands' harbors. Harbor dues are charged for ships entering and transferring their catches and in 1983 brought in revenues amounting to £¼ million.

However, the Falklands at present only have a three-mile limit which gives no opportunity to license or to control the actual fishing.

At the time of the 1976 Shackleton Report, tourism on a

small scale was already in operation and showing its potential. Three forms of tourism were developing, one exclusively from Argentines visiting from their natural curiosity and their desire to shop for British goods; a second form involving a minimal number of tourist vessels which call at the Falklands as part of a more extensive cruise to Antarctica; finally a semispecialist operation revolving around the Falklands' unique wildlife attractions. This latter form was appearing to have the best long-term possibilities, with the Islands slowly developing the name of the Galápagos of the South Atlantic. However, by virtue of their geographical location and the more constraining environment, this type of tourism would probably not have developed beyond the specialist type of wildlife enthusiast.

In the light of the recent conflict, most tourism except for a limited number of visits by cruise vessels going to Antarctica has ceased, due to the break in communications with Argentina. The whole development program as suggested in the Shackleton Report also had to be reviewed. When the Falklands' conflict was being fought and it was evident that Britain intended to regain her territory, Lord Shackleton was asked by the British government to update his earlier report on the Islands. This he and his team did and the revised report was published in September, 1982. Shackleton in his second report reiterated the point that the Islands were still almost totally dependent upon the production and export of wool and that the economy was in danger of serious contraction and possibly even a final collapse. He again emphasized the importance of establishing small owner occupied farms and the setting up of a Falkland Islands Development Agency which would buy some of the larger estates for the purpose of subdivision. The intention then would be to sell or lease or make available to local people who were willing to take on the responsibility of working them and thus make their livelihoods in the Falklands.

Since the publication of the revised report, the subdivision of land has been intensified and by late 1983 three large estates had been purchased by the Falkland Islands government and divided into smaller farming units. Shackleton in the revised report also recommended the setting up of a pilot project in salmon ranching, experimental offshore fishing, and a local knitwear industry, but emphasized that the re-establishment of a regular air link with the Islands was crucial to all the proposals.

At the close of the conflict an air link was imperative for the speedy resupply of the garrison. Using Ascension Island as a staging point, an "air-bridge" was quickly established between Britain and the Falkland Islands, using Hercules transport aircraft and a system of in-flight refueling on the 3,800-mile stretch between Ascension Island and Port Stanley. Ships also make their way between the same points, continually bringing in machinery and supplies for the large garrison now established in the Islands. Although these lines of communication are very largely for the British forces, islanders are carried in and out of the colony. Due to the sensitive nature of the Falklands-Argentina situation, the one-time link with other South American countries, such as Chile, Uruguay, and Brazil, is not used and islanders either fly or make a sea voyage directly to England via Ascension Island. This is an odd twist, placing us back in the times when the Falklands were remote and isolated from the rest of the world.

Stanley Airport built by Britain at the cost of £4½ million.

The present airport, at Cape Pembroke, built at a cost of some £4.5 million and opened in December, 1977, was large enough to accommodate the type of jets used for the service between the South American mainland and the Falklands. However, for the type of jet needed to make the long flight from Ascension Island, a much larger runway is required. In 1983 the British government announced its intentions of building a much larger strategic airport at a cost of £215 million, for use by the Ministry of Defense. To be constructed some miles south of Stanley at Mount Pleasant, the runway will be designed to take the heavier, long-haul type jets. Although basically a military installation, it is expected that the new airport, to be operational by early 1985, will play a dual role, taking commercial aircraft also.

The Shackleton Report had proposed in its first publication the spending of some £13 to £14 million for development of the Islands, but prior to the conflict of 1982, little action had been taken on these recommendations. The second report proposed an expenditure of some £30 to £35 million and shortly after the liberation the British government announced that £31 million would be made available for development over a period of five years. Apart from this development aid, a further £15 million was made available for the rehabilitation of the Islands following the "war." With this aid a new internal air service has been established to replace what was lost in the conflict. New houses are under construction. Roads and public services are being renewed. All these things were needed by the Islands in any case, but it is indeed sad that a "war" was the moving factor.

The action of the invasion by Argentina, followed by the occupation and the subsequent retaking of the Islands by Britain, have all brought change. Islanders, who knew nothing but peace, a relaxed, quiet life, and a pace perhaps out of line with the rest of the world, have suddenly been presented with the reverse. The islanders themselves, as we have seen, are very adaptable in a practical sense. Many, such as the young, wanted to see the pace of life speeded up and they will probably adapt. But there will be many others who are finding they have lost that very special way of life which has, until the present time, kept them in the Islands. Actually to analyze and put into words what this means is very difficult, for there is more to life in the Falklands than the points already mentioned. The environment alone is important and, although rigorous at times, it has a very special attraction for many. In different ways it presents a challenge and emphasizes the pioneering spirit which holds many people to the Islands. It has avoided the clamor of modern life and can still claim to hear the silence, especially in the Camp.

One of the main factors concerning the future of the Falkland Islands and their people has been the sovereignty dispute. Proposals were put forward for the possible solving of the dispute and these were rejected. But I ask myself if there are not other ways in which these rather unique islands should have the peace and security they deserve.

While the Falklands remained comparatively obscure and isolated from the rest of the world and its inhabitants were prepared to adopt a simple life-style, it seemed that the natural environment was becoming increasingly important as an integral part of that life. The environment and its wildlife were attaining the recognition they deserved; gradually it was being realized that such things were now rare in the world and were an important asset to the Falklands. Specialized wildlife tourism had become increasingly important over the ten years or so in which it had been in operation up until the 1982 conflict.

Perhaps the most significant achievement was the increasing number of suggestions being made in many places, including Argentina, that the solution to the Falklands problem could be found through its wildlife. Was it not possible, for example, that the Falklands could be turned into some form of international wildlife reserve, with the islanders as trustees? The prestige alone of such a move in the eyes of the world would surely have been tremendous and could even have been a viable scheme. Now, however, the Falklands have experienced a war and there have been changes. At the present time we have a situation which has become known as "Fortress Falklands," and behind this there is the overpowering call for sudden "development" of the Islands. Hopefully this can be guided in the right direction and the importance of the natural environment taken into account.

In the long term there has to be an alternative to "Fortress Falklands" and for this to happen there must eventually be a return to peaceful relations with Argentina. What the final solution might be to the sovereignty issue, which seems to be a prerequisite for normal relations with Argentina, is at

Fortunately, unaffected by the conflict, gentoo and rockhopper penguins return to breed on the Islands.

Colony of albatrosses and penguins on a Falkland reserve. Without careful thought for their future such sights could possibly vanish from the Islands.

present not clear. Before the conflict there were suggestions for some form of lease-back arrangement, whereby sovereignty might have been ceded to Argentina, with Great Britain taking back a lease. This solution now seems remote. Perhaps some sort of trusteeship under the United Nations is another possible answer.

Returning to the international reserve proposal, is it not possible that the Antarctic Treaty could be extended to include the Falklands, thus freezing claims to sovereignty and, more importantly, demilitarize the area? I also believe that another possibility lies in the World Heritage Convention. This was convened in 1972 and now has some sixty-five signatories, including Argentina. The convention is managed by the director general of the United Nations Education and Scientific Organization, protecting areas of the world of outstanding natural and cultural value. The Great Barrier Reef and the Galápagos Islands are protected by the convention; why not the Falkland Islands? In the years that I have lived in the Islands studying their wildlife and traveling to the more remote areas of the archipelago, I have learned that they are a very special part of this world; they are unique for their wildlife; they are also very delicate in environmental terms. Can they stand what we are doing to them at the present time in the defense of principles? It is claimed that time heals wounds; we can only hope that wounds are healed quickly, for the longer the present situation exists the more danger there is of a wound that may never heal being inflicted on the Falkland Islands' delicate environment.

The author, naturalist, artist, and conservationist.

Selected list of scientific names of animals and plants common to the Falkland Islands

Falkland Fox or Warrah *Dusicyon antarcticus australis*

Falkland Fur Seal *Arctocephalus australis australis*

Southern Sea Lion *Otaria byronia*

Southern Elephant Seal *Mirounga leonina*

Leopard Seal *Hydrurga leptonyx*

Sperm Whale *Physeter catadon*

Sei Whale *Balaenoptera borealis*

Humpback Whale *Megaptera novaeangliae*

Blue Whale *Balaenoptera musculus*

Fin Whale *Balaenoptera physalus*

Killer Whale *Orcinus orca*

Lobster Krill *Munida* sp.

Basket Kelp *Macrocystis pyrifera*

Tree Kelp *Lessoniae* sp.

Durvillea Kelp *Durvillea antarctica*

Lettuce Kelp *Ulva* sp.

Tussock Grass *Poa flabellata*

White Grass *Cortaderia pilosa*

Balsam Bog *Bolax gummifera*

Diddle-dee *Empetrum rubrum*

Small Fern *Blechnum penna marina*

Blechnum Fern *Blechnum tabulare*

Teaberry *Myrteola nummularia*

Native Strawberry *Rubus geoides*

King Penguin *Aptenodytes patagonica*

Gentoo Penguin *Pygoscelis papua*

Rockhopper Penguin *Eudyptes crestatus*

Macaroni Penguin *Eudyptes chrysolophus*

Magellan Penguin *Spheniscus magellanicus*

Rolland's Grebe *Podiceps rolland*

Silver Grebe *Podiceps occipitalis*

Black-browed Albatross *Diomedea melanophrys*

Giant Petrel *Macronectes giganteus*

Thin-billed Prion *Pachyptila belcheri*

F.Is. Fairy Prion *Pachyptila turtur*

White-chinned Petrel *Procellaria aequinoctialis*

Sooty Shearwater *Puffinus griseus*

Greater Shearwater *Puffinus gravis*

Wilson's Petrel *Oceanites oceanicus*

Gray-backed Storm Petrel *Garrodia nereis*

Falkland Diving Petrel *Pelecanoides urinatrix berard*

Rock Shag *Phalacrocorax magellanicus*

King Shag   *Phalacrocorax atriceps albiventer*

Night Heron   *Nycticorax n. cyanocephalus*

Ruddy-headed Goose   *Chloephaga rubidiceps*

Upland Goose   *Chloephaga picta leucoptera*

Ashy-headed Goose   *Chloephaga poliocephala*

Kelp Goose   *Chloephaga hybrida malvinarum*

Black-necked Swan   *Cygnus melanocoryphus*

Crested (Gray) Duck   *Anas cristata*

Cinnamon Teal   *Anas cyanoptera*

Chiloe Widgeon   *Anas sibilatrix*

Yellow-billed Teal   *Anas flavrirostris*

Brown Pintail   *Anas spinicauda*

Pampa Teal   *Anas versicolor*

Flightless Steamer Duck   *Tachyeres brachypterus*

Flying Steamer Duck   *Tachyeres patachonicus*

Turkey Vulture   *Cathartes aura jota*

Striated Caracara, "Johnny Rook"   *Phalcoboenus australis*

Crested Caracara   *Polyborus plancus*

Red-backed Hawk   *Buteo polyosoma*

Pied (Fuegian) Oystercatcher   *Haematopus leucopodus*

Black Oystercatcher   *Haematopus ater*

Falkland Island Plover   *Charadrius falklandicus*

Winter Plover (Dotterel)   *Zonibyx modestus*

Common Snipe   *Gallinago gallinago*

South American Tern   *Sterna hirundinacea*

Brown-hooded Gull   *Larus maculipennis*

Dominican Gull   *Larus dominicanus*

Magellan (Dolphin) Gull   *Leucophaeus scoresbii*

Skua   *Catharacta skua antarctica*

Short-eared Owl   *Asio flammeus sanfordi*

Barn Owl   *Tyto alba*

Tussock Bird   *Cinclodes antarcticus*

Dark-faced Ground-tyrant   *Muscisaxicola m. macloviana*

Grass Wren   *Cistothorus platensis falklandicus*

Cobb's Wren   *Troglodytes aedon cobbi*

Falkland Thrush   *Turdus f. falklandii*

Falkland Pipit   *Anthus correndera grayi*

Military Starling   *Sturnella loyca falklandica*

Siskin   *Spinus barbatus*

Black-throated Finch   *Melanodera m. melanodera*

House Sparrow   *Passer domesticus*

INDEX